£10

THE THREEFOLD REALITY

By the same author

INTO GOD

THE WAY INTO GOD

HUMAN NEEDS IN MODERN SOCIETY

(with B. T. Reynolds)

THE THREEFOLD REALITY

An Exercise in Contemplation

R. G. COULSON

I AM thy Shield, and thy Exceeding Great Reward.
GEN. 15,1.

I AM thy Portion and thine Inheritance.
NUM. 18,20 RV.

I AM God . . . the Holy One in the midst of thee.
HOS. 11,9.

First published in 1966
Copyright by R. G. Coulson

Printed in Great Britain by Sparta Press (Blackfen) Ltd.,
Westwood Lane, Sidcup, Kent.

Contents

Preface

The object of this book is ultimately practical, in spite of any contrary impression its title may create. It is to understand more perfectly the Reality and man's place and purpose therein, in order to pursue that purpose more perfectly. Anyone who has seriously tried to study the problem of the Reality will probably agree that it can never be finally solved. For the Reality is boundless. The student has therefore to select a point at which to set out the results of his studies, however incomplete they may be. Such a point may well be one towards the end of his earthly life, when his experience is at its widest, while at the same time his capacity to rationalise it is still unimpaired. Such a point best serves the interests, not only of the author in preparing him for the approaching change in his life, but of his fellow-workers in helping them to carry on their common work.

An aim of this description may seem to be so far beyond the scope of any short book as to render it unworthy of serious notice. The best hope of dispelling such an adverse impression is to indicate the origin of this book. Though written by one person, which is necessary for the sake of clarity, its authorship is essentially corporate. It is the result of many divergent views, religious as well as secular, which have been drawn together into a coherent whole in the course of some eighteen years' study. Various groups have shared in this study, the most important contribution being made by one composed of Anglican clergy. During that period the membership of these widely diverse groups has both changed and increased. Hence the corporate view here set out is not the formally agreed result of all who have contributed to it. The view can properly be fathered only on the author, who alone knows everyone who has made any contribution towards it. He alone is responsible for working out and presenting the result of the corporate experience, study and practice, including its undoubted errors of matter and manner of presentation. In this sense the view is his own.

It is necessary to give some indication of the corporate experience, study and practice which have gone to produce this view. To begin with the corporate experience; this was mainly gained in the course of regularly recurring retreats, which were at the same time fairly strenuous contemplative exercises. Any retreat conductor who seeks to express the Holy Spirit and not his own must be aware of his debt to those who share in the retreat; for he thereby receives enormously more than he passes on. In order to express ideas that are put into his mind, he is obliged to clarify them. So he draws out profounder ideas that are banked up in his unconscious depths and which in their turn have to be clarified, until he finds himself informed by ideas whose subsistence he never knew, and which he is unable to express. At that point his meditation may be transcended by spiritual experience, the universal substance of all thought. Here may begin the contemplative silence which is the best condition for experience still farther beyond expression. The conductor's experience is directly communicated to the others present, and theirs to him, and so *together* they penetrate to the ineffable Spiritual Ground of all things at a greater depth than is usually possible *alone*.

The deeper any experience is, the more it sooner or later calls for rationalisation. Therefore, the corporate experience gained in retreats, and of course renewed individually in between, inevitably stimulated discussion and study. This soon confirmed that such experience was not exclusively Christian and that conventional Christian theology alone could not adequately rationalise it. It became necessary to draw on other religious traditions. Further consideration revealed that the experience could not be rationalised in exclusively religious terms, but involved philosophy, art and science. It became plain that if the experience concerned the Spiritual Ground of all things, no serious attempt at rationalisation could ignore any aspect of genuine knowledge. Furthermore, no attempt was worth making without complete freedom, not only outer but inner, to follow the argument withersoever it led.

Then arose the problem of correlating the various aspects of knowledge into a coherent scheme of the Reality and of man's place and purpose therein. The scheme had to include all aspects without distorting any. Since man's deepest and most intensive spiritual knowledge recorded in the Scriptures underlies the various religious traditions, these had to form the base of the scheme. At the same time man's widest and most extensive corporeal knowledge

recorded in the disciplines which underlie the various secular traditions had to fit upon that base. And the base had to carry the
superstructure without distorting either.

This problem led to another at least as big. It became evident
that if these various aspects of knowledge continued to be understood in conventional terms alone, they could not be fitted together
without distortion. If the Scriptures were to provide the unifying
basis of the scheme, they above all required to be understood at
a deeper level than the conventional. What was to guarantee the
soundness of any such understanding, that it was in fact deeper
and not merely more fanciful? Its essential agreement with the
traditional views seemed the best guarantee. If the new was rooted
in the old and grew out of it, which is the universal pattern of all
growth, then it might claim to be deeper understanding. For it
then had a claim to fulfil and not destroy the old.[1]

However carefully this work was done, the resulting view of the
Reality and man's place and purpose therein could not be regarded
as more than a hypothesis. Its truth had therefore to be subjected
to the test of practical application. How far did this hypothesis
stand up to this test? More exactly, how far did this scheme of
the Reality and of man's place and purpose therein persuade anyone,
made aware of these problems by experience, seriously to pursue that
purpose? Those who contributed to the hypothesis have undoubtedly been so persuaded. They have been persuaded according to
the depth of their spiritual experience and the amount of work
they have put into its rationalisation. Have others been persuaded?
Many have, and as always they have been persuaded only in the
degree that their spiritual experience has presented them with problems and they have themselves tried to work out their solution.

Enough has perhaps been said to indicate the corporate origin
of this book, and one may hope that the view it expresses may at
least appear worthy of proper examination. When all is said, however, the view will convince only in so far as it answers questions
which the reader himself is more or less explicitly asking.

Having touched on the matter with which this book is concerned,
the manner in which it is presented cannot be left out. The title,
The Threefold Reality, may appear to imply a good deal of technical theological, philosophical and scientific language. But in fact

[1]Mat. 5, 17.

the simplest possible language has been used throughout, for the following reason. Whoever wishes fully to convey ideas to another must try to express them so that they may be not only thought about but put into practice. For only then can they be so fully understood as to be possessed. Now the profounder ideas are, the easier they are to express in abstract language. But the more abstract this is, the harder it is to put into practice. If the abstractions are not to remain mere food for thought but are also to be put into practice, they need to be translated into simple concrete terms. Hence spiritual literature is usually simple in the degree that it is spiritually "technical".

Since the ideas this book tries to express concern the Reality, they could not be more profound, nor more difficult to put into practice in order to be understood so fully as to be possessed. They therefore need to be expressed in the simplest possible language. Which the author has tried to do, however unsuccessfully. Words have been italicised to convey meaning in preference to longer statements. The Divine has been distinguished from the human by the use of capitals. This has been done even when quoting actual Bible texts. (These are all taken from the Authorised Version, except when otherwise stated). In the result the language of this book is sometimes perhaps deceptively simple.

The author can never properly thank all who have shared in the corporate experience, study and practice which underlie the view he puts forward. They have carried him with them towards an awareness of the Reality which he never imagined possible. He must thank all others, too numerous to acknowledge in detail, who by their written or spoken views of the Reality have consciously or unconsciously contributed to this awareness. He is no less indebted to his opponents in thought, feeling and action. For their opposition, and not least when it has been hostile, has saved him from stagnation and thus added both depth and breadth to his awareness. Above all he must thank his wife, not only for her help in the course of writing this book, but for her careful checking of the manuscript.

R.G.C.

PART I

Chapter I

Introduction

[1]

The author hopes that the reader will think with him, and in due course act with him, and therefore adopts the third person plural in setting out his views. Let us begin by assuming that every normal human being more or less consciously seeks that which appears good, beautiful and true to him, and which he therefore regards as most real, and that he tries to arrange his life in pursuit of its attainment. To him this is the Reality. The fact that some men deliberately avoid the Reality only proves their awareness of it. Since no two men's insight and capacity are wholly alike, that which appears real to one man may appear illusory to another. Necessarily therefore innumerable schemes of the Reality have been formulated and acted upon throughout history.

But though no two men are wholly alike, all men in some degree think, feel and act. The schemes of the Reality that are formulated thus tend to fall into three separate main categories, each being dominated by thought, or by feeling, or by activity. On the other hand, thinking, feeling and activity are but three aspects of one more or less integrated self. Therefore these three approaches to the Reality are never wholly unrelated to each other, and attempts are constantly made to unite them in a synthesis.

The degree of success achieved by these attempts indicates the degree of integration or wholeness possessed by those who formulate, and by those who accept, these schemes of the Reality. It measures the depth, breadth and clarity of their vision of the Reality, and determines the effectiveness of their pursuit of it.

The twentieth century version of this universal pattern is especially clear. In this period the three main approaches to the Reality just mentioned seem to be clearly represented by what may be called the religious, the secular and the specifically humanist stand-

11

points. By the latter we mean a standpoint which is humanist in its own right, as it were, independently of the religious and secular ones. Though not wholly unrelated to each other, they appear to be more distinct from each other than in almost any previous age. The result is that many intelligent people above subsistence level tend to be without any coherent vision of the Reality. They see no ultimate purpose in their own life, or indeed in human existence in general.

They thus spend themselves in the pursuit of every conceivable lesser purpose. None of these can of course yield them more than lesser satisfactions. They are, in other words, fundamentally distracted, dissatisfied and frustrated. As they blunder along a confused course, which they themselves recognise as having no ultimate end, the future can hardly fail to appear problematical to them. Their uncertainty thus becomes increasingly fearful. Since they are on the whole the leaders of western civilisation, from which all civilisation on this earth is at present taking its cue, their malaise seems destined to spread to all terrestrial mankind.

The reader will probably be too familiar with the present malaise to require a detailed diagnosis of it.[1] He is more likely to be interested in the cure of the all-too familiar disease. Any cure must clearly include at least two essentials. The first is a synthesis of the religious, the secular and the humanist approaches to the Reality in a single coherent scheme. The other is some practical method of ordering life in pursuit of the Reality, here and now. This book is an attempt to contribute towards the discussion of such a two-fold cure which involves both theory and practice.

Let us introduce our discussion on a positive note. It is the keynote of all that follows. The present malaise is not to be deplored as essentially a disaster, however great the suffering it may involve or threaten. For it must be regarded as an inevitable phase in man's progress towards his attainment of the greatest possible degree of the Reality. And in relation to such an end the present malaise can only be counted negligible. It is indeed due to no more than the decay of an outgrown scheme of that Reality, the fulness of which it is man's destiny to attain. The malaise is the birth-pain of a deeper, broader and clearer vision.

---

[1] Among others it is dealt with in the author's books mentioned on the flyleaf.

Such a positive view of the prevailing malaise may appear rather facile, perhaps even callous. Later chapters should show it as being sound from a theological, philosophical and psychological standpoint. But it may call for some justification even in this introductory chapter. Those who study history as a record of man's pursuit of the Reality and the corresponding satisfaction of self-fulfilment will recognise that his vision of the Reality has repeatedly disintegrated. His life has then lost its order and purpose, and he has suffered accordingly. The crucial question is: why does his vision disintegrate? A priori, we must expect this for the same reason that any other achieved result disintegrates. Without such disintegration further development, leading to still greater results, would be impossible. We now have the key to what actually happens.

The deeper, broader and clearer any vision of the Reality is, the more self-fulfilment it must lead to. In other words, man attains some measure of the Reality and enjoys the corresponding degree of satisfaction. Having done so, he inevitably relaxes. The effect of this tends to make him take the consequent blessings for granted, cease to value them, and complacently fancy himself fully adequate and self-sufficient. In other words, he acts as though he had already attained the ultimate Reality and complete self-fulfilment.[1]

This delusion amounts to a distortion of man's vision of the Reality. He thus strays off his true course in its pursuit, inevitably blunders into difficulties, and suffers accordingly. The farther and longer he strays off his true course, the more he suffers both inwardly and outwardly. Hence human suffering is repeatedly liable to approach the point of mortal agony. This critical point is not naturally tolerable. Therefore, as the crisis approaches, so does the moment at which man returns to his pursuit of a greater Reality than his own still imperfect and deficient self.

He finds, of course, in the degree that he truly seeks. Just as to take a breath is to fill the lungs with the all-pervading air. But the vision that he regains cannot be the same as that which was lost. For he himself is no longer the same as he was. His

---

[1] Among other things, the Bible is a profound record of human experience, and as such mentions repeated instances of this delusion, e.g. Deut. 8,11-14; Hos. 13,6.

intervening suffering, and his renewed search forced on him by his suffering, and intensified thereby, lead him to a correspondingly deeper and broader and clearer vision than before. Just as the deeper a man breathes, the more air he takes into his lungs. More exactly, the scheme of the Reality which he reformulates is a fuller, richer and more comprehensive synthesis than before. Having achieved this at cost to himself, in terms relevant to his stature increased by suffering, and in that sense his own work, he correspondingly values the Reality he has rediscovered. He therefore pursues it with relevant zeal.

Each crisis thus marks a step in man's chequered progress towards the fulfilment of his ultimate purpose. Human development, individual and collective, is no more possible without crisis than any other growth which, as we have seen, must involve the break-up of the old for the sake of the greater new. The stable periods between crises are as the winter sleep during which all creation stores up the powers for summer growth.

The spiral pattern of this dialectical process is no doubt familiar enough as a philosophical theory. It must be a good deal less familiar as an experienced fact. Otherwise suffering, and the evil it springs from and engenders, would not pose the problems they commonly do.

[2]

If this book is to contribute anything worth-while towards a synthesis of the three approaches to the Reality which are more distinct in this age than ever before, if it is to make any useful contribution towards the formulation of a new and richer scheme of the Reality, and especially to a way of pressing on to the attainment of a greater measure of Reality than hitherto, the spiral pattern of the dialectical process we have just outlined will have to be reduced to more concrete terms than we have used. We shall have to trace the pattern as it repeats itself, not merely in history in general, but in our age. Without this, the terms in which our scheme of the Reality comes to be formulated will lack relevance. Worse still, the spiritual training that is to be suggested for the pursuit of the Reality will violate one of the most basic principles governing such exercises. This principle demands that, though rooted in the universality of the eternal, such exercises must be clearly applicable in some particular situation in time. In order to bring out the essence of the present situation for our purpose this outline will of course have to be extremely crude.

Since the dialectical pattern of human development we have mentioned is on the whole an ascending spiral, we may fix the beginning of the cycle we choose for examination at whatever point is most convenient. We will choose the point where the scheme of the Reality was last clearly formulated as a coherent whole, and its attainment pursued as the ultimate end in human existence. And since it looks as though the predominantly active westerner may lead the rest of terrestrial mankind in the next few generations, we will confine that point to his ancestral home, Europe. This point is the one that may be loosely called the mediaeval age of faith.

The coherent vision of the Reality in this age, and the consequent synthesis of thinking, feeling and activity, naturally released a corresponding concentration of human vitality which led to the age of progress, the Renaissance. Its spiritual impetus ran down in the eighteenth century, when the cycle slowed to a standstill in a stable situation. The scheme of the Reality was generally, though not of course anything like unanimously, accepted as three-tiered. It may perhaps be summed up as follows without undue distortion. In heaven above was God as Creator Spirit. On earth below was man as the summit of creation, which existed for his use. Between these heavenly and earthly extremes, and partaking of both, was the Son of God Who as both God and man was the essential link between these two opposites. And the purpose of all creation, and therefore predominantly of man's existence, as its summit, was to glorify God. More precisely, man was created to serve God according to his individual and collective capacity. Service thus varied from manual work to spiritual worship for the Glory of God through the mediation of His Son. Its reward was the enjoyment of everlasting life in heaven through the Son of God. Its effect on earth was to be the building of the City of God through the Church of God.

This coherent conception of the Reality, approximately unifying men's thinking, feeling and active aspects, was naturally reflected in a correspondingly ordered pyramidal structure of society. Its peak was represented by authoritarian monarchies, its base by the tractable masses, and the essential link between these extremes and partaking of both were the aristocracies.

As usual, however, the blessings of the stability yielded by an age of faith and consequent progress were soon taken for granted. Characteristically, uninterrupted human progress came to be regarded as assured, and in the nineteenth century even as automatic. Its source and ground in a coherent vision of the Reality was forgotten. God as the spiritual peak of the Reality appeared less necessary to man. Whatever theoretical importance was still accorded to God in the twentieth century, by the majority of men, in practice for them man became "the measure of all things". The divinity of the link between God and man lost most of its point, and the Son of God was allowed little more than his humanity. For all practical purposes therefore the threefold scheme of the Reality became reduced to its third, its earthly, term alone; that is to say, man and the universe in their corporeal aspect. With its spiritual aspect at its peak thus for practical purposes abandoned, the scheme became grossly distorted, and human existence largely lost any convincing ultimate purpose.

Such a distorted scheme was bound to collapse. And so the body of human thinking, feeling and activity disintegrated into three virtually unrelated standpoints. Each, no longer balanced by the others, became dominated by one of these three main human approaches to the Reality. Thought generated a standpoint which was in essence mainly secular, feeling one which was mainly religious, and activity one which was mainly humanist.

The disintegration continued within each standpoint. Thought split into modes which became mutually exclusive as deductive and inductive. Each developed along its own lines, continuing to split into ever greater detail, losing touch with its roots and with its collaterals, until the thinking man in the twentieth century is said to know more and more about less and less. Human experience, in so far as it was conditioned by thought, disintegrated into an increasing variety of unrelated fields, each becoming correspondingly shallow. And human activity thus split into a growing mass of unrelated lesser ends.

The result of this vertical and horizontal disintegration is that the body of human thought, feeling and activity has split into the three separate secular, religious and specifically humanist approaches to the Reality. The mass of western men in the twentieth century think, feel and act far more diversely than their predecessors. But their vision of the Reality as a whole is far less clear than before. They therefore feel far less strongly moved to seek any ultimate end in their life, and are correspondingly frustrated. Pursuing so many more unrelated diverse ends than before, they are necessarily far less satisfied than before. For the more unrelated ends there are, the more liable they are to conflict with one another, not only in individual men but in society. The satisfaction of successfully pursuing them is thus correspondingly rare. And even when attained, being lesser ends, the satisfactions they yield are lesser too. In other words, human suffering has greatly increased.

The disintegration of the scheme of the Reality commonly accepted in the age of faith, and the consequent frustration, dissatisfaction and suffering have inevitably been reflected in the growing instability of the social structure. For man builds this consciously or unconsciously according to his vision of the Reality, as the objective counterpart of the latter. The French Revolution gave it its first serious jolt. Further shocks occurred throughout the nineteenth century, in the course of which the sovereignty vested in monarchs came to be increasingly shared, not only by the aristocracies as before, but by the middle classes. In the twentieth century sovereignty is in process of being shared by the masses in general. It is as though the peak of the social pyramid, which has been expanding downwards, now collapsed onto its base. So the pyramid is reduced to a formless heap to match the disintegrating vision of the Reality of which it is an embodiment. In the second half of the twentieth century there is no clearly defined structure of society at all.

If the social structure is an embodiment of the prevailing vision of the Reality, one would expect disintegration to produce comparable gains and losses in both cases. Hence we find that the collapse of the social pyramid has left its component individuals far more free, distinctive and diverse than before. But they are paying for this gain with at least as much suffering as the disintegration of their vision of the Reality has cost them. We may say that the subjective aspect of their suffering is now amplified by its objective counterpart.

[3]

The more intelligent, sensitive and active people are of course the first to react to suffering. The traditionalists among them tend to regard the malaise that causes it as a disaster. What they essentially seek therefore is a restoration of the broken scheme of the Reality, of the lost social structure that embodies it, and of the consequent blessings that have departed. For radicals the malaise is a goad to further destructive change. But those who regard the malaise as birth-pain seek the constructive change needed to formulate a fresh scheme of the Reality and to build a richer social structure than before. They look for blessings of a higher order than were generally possible before. As the essential first step, they seek a synthesis of the religious, secular and humanist standpoints in a deeper, wider and clearer vision of the Reality, followed by a closer integration of human thought, feeling and activity in pursuit of the Reality than before.

We have a pointer towards this synthesis if we recall the gains produced by the decay of the previous one. We saw that, whatever depth, width and clarity was lost when the body of thought, feeling and activity split into three separate categories, each was freed from its parent synthesis to develop along its own lines. Each has thus gained in precision, variety and intensity. If these one-sided but more penetrating approaches to the Reality can be reconciled in a new synthesis, this will represent a correspondingly deeper, wider and clearer vision than the lost one. The resulting social structure, its components having been liberated by the collapse of the previous one for further individual development, will be that much richer. So will the consequent blessings enjoyed by its members.

In this synthesis of the three approaches the religious one would be primarily concerned with the unitive, universal spiritual aspect of the Reality, but also contain the *outline* of its corporeal counterpart. The secular approach would be primarily concerned with the multiple, particularised corporeal aspect of the Reality, but also contain the *substance* of its spiritual archetype. And the humanist approach would be concerned with the relationships between these subjective-objective opposites, in order to understand, possess and use the corporeal in the light of the spiritual for the greatest possible human self-fulfilment. Since each of these three approaches is that of human beings, a spiritually enlightened humanism equally concerned with both the spiritual and corporeal aspects of the Reality would be able to integrate all three in a rich synthesis.

Spiritually united with each other, human beings could afford to differ in their thinking, feeling and activity in the corporeal realm as much as they chose. Understanding the changeless principles underlying all changing things, they could apply them for their individual and corporate self-fulfilment in endless variety without confusion. There seems to be no other way of building a social structure in which all men who are aware of being selves can together take the next great step towards the attainment of the ultimate Reality.

Having given what appears to us to be the most fruitful approach to the new synthesis, it remains for us to indicate the result of our own attempt to formulate a scheme of the Reality and of man's place and purpose therein. If it is placed beside its outworn predecessor, its significance should stand out, not as a novelty, but as an unfoldment of the old. This, as we have seen, is an indispensable guarantee of its soundness. Since the rest of this book is concerned with this subject, all we need, or can, do here is to introduce its barest outline.

We have seen the previous scheme to have been somewhat in the following terms. In heaven above was God as Creator Spirit. Below was corporeal man as the summit of creation which existed for his use. Between these opposites, partaking of both and thus linking them, was the Divine-human Son of God. The purpose of human existence was to work for the Glory of God according to individual capacity, through the mediation of His Son. Service thus varied from manual work to spiritual worship to the Glory of God. Its reward was the enjoyment of everlasting life in heaven through the Son of God.

Since this scheme was conceived mainly in religious terms, humanism playing a minor part in it and secularism hardly any, our first task is to choose fresh terms in which to re-state it. The more universal and abstract they are (without being unintelligible at this stage), the more properly they will express a scheme which includes humanist and secularist as well as religious attitudes. We need no more than touch on the reasons for our choice of terms here because the next chapter will clarify them.

We begin by translating the three main terms of the previous scheme, God, Son of God and Man, into three chief aspects of the Reality. Stated dynamically, these are the chief degrees of the manifestation, expression, unfoldment of the Whole Reality. The first corresponds with God, and is Absolute, Eternal, Infinite. It is super-personal and super-essential and therefore super-intelligible. It is unknowable. Hidden in "Itself", the Reality here is not manifested, expressed, unfolded at all. This is the ultimate Source, Ground and Goal of all that is or can be knowable.

The second aspect and degree of the Reality corresponds with the Son of God, and represents the unfoldment of the infinite in spiritual terms. The second comprises all that is or can be spiritually knowable. It is therefore spiritually personal. Here the hidden Glory of the infinite Reality is unfolded in spiritual terms as spiritual Goodness, Beauty and Truth. More precisely, being personal, as The SELF Who is spiritually Good, Beautiful and True. Since He is the total spiritual manifestation, expression, unfoldment of The Infinite, He has been truly called The Word of God as well as The Son.

The third aspect or degree of the Reality corresponds with Man and represents the unfoldment of the spiritual in corporeal terms. The third comprises all that is or can be corporeally knowable. It is therefore corporeally personal. Here the spiritual Reality, the Goodness, Beauty and Truth of The SELF, is unfolded in corporeal terms, down to their outermost conditions of space, time and change. More precisely, The SELF Who is spiritually Good, Beautiful and True unfolds Himself in selves who are corporeally good, beautiful and true. Space, time and change being what they are, the unitive, universal spiritual Goodness, Beauty and Truth of His SELF can only be expressed in such terms by an endless multitude and diversity of corporeally good, beautiful and true selves.

The above translation makes it plain that the "heaven" and "earth" of the old scheme are now best rendered as the "spiritual realm" and the "corporeal realm" respectively.

It remains for us to re-state the purpose of human existence in terms which could be equally relevant and significant for the religious, the secular and the humanist standpoints. According to the old view, all men exist for the purpose of working and worshipping to the Glory of God and thereby glorifying God on earth through the mediation of His Son. Their reward is the enjoyment of ever-lasting life through Him in heaven. We re-state this as follows. All corporeal selves exist to manifest, express, unfold in spatio-temporal terms the Goodness, Beauty and Truth of their archetype, The Spiritual SELF. Even as He subsists to manifest, express, unfold in spiritual terms by these supreme values the hidden Glory of The Infinite beyond all. So through The Spiritual SELF all corporeal selves unfold in spatio-temporal terms the hidden Glory of the infinite Reality, and thereby attain Infinity themselves. This is the ultimate purpose of their existence and their supreme destiny.

No greater destiny is possible or indeed conceivable for corporeal selves. For it means that their whole corporeal nature and environment are destined to shine forth with the perfect Goodness, Beauty and Truth which is the Glory of the infinite Reality. They are destined to know in themselves, and thus to incarnate, the infinite Reality.[1] It must therefore be that all selves are destined ultimately to think, feel and act in the corporeal realm according to The SELF in the spiritual, and through Him according to The Infinite beyond all.[2]

Thought, feeling and action seem hardly predicable of The SELF, and not at all of The Infinite. Yet men of most of the great religious traditions have recorded experiences in which the Divine Mind, Heart and Will are expressly referred to.[3] Those of the Hebrew and Christian traditions mention explicit promises of The Infinite to dwell in men and to walk in them.[4] There is evidence of the fulfilment of the promise in various degrees, up to the supreme.[5]

At the risk of labouring the point, it may be of help if we correlate the three great approaches to the Reality in the more practical terms we have just used. The religious approach would be concerned with ever deeper union with the endlessly rich Mind, Heart and Will of The SELF with a view to illuminating the corresponding facets of corporeal selves. The secular approach would be concerned with the ever wider development of the endlessly diverse thoughts, feelings and activities of selves in the light of these facets

---

[1] E.g. 2 Cor. 6,16; 1 Jn. 2,23.
[2] As far of course as Infinity is expressible in corporeal terms.
[3] E.g. 1 Sam. 2,35; Isa. 55,8; Jn. 1,13 in the Bible.
[4] Lev. 26,12 as interpreted in 2 Cor. 6,16.
[5] E.g. Jn. 1,14; Col. 2,9.

of The Spiritual SELF. And the humanist approach, recognising the complementary nature and value of selfhood, would work for the ever closer correspondence between the facets in their spiritual and corporeal aspects. The three approaches integrated in one would thus be able to bring about corporeal man's next great step towards the fulfilment of his destiny. This is to unfold, by the integrated diversity of his thinking, feeling and activity, a greater measure than before of the endlessly rich Goodness, Beauty and Truth of his spiritual archetype, and thus to show forth corporeally a corresponding measure of the infinite Reality.

[4]

We see then that the crisis gathering momentum in the second half of the twentieth century challenges man with increasing insistence to brace himself for the next great step towards ultimate self-fulfilment. Enough has been said to show that this step involves nothing less than deliberate and systematic training in fitness to incarnate man's spiritual archetype, and through Him The Infinite.

The sages, mystics and saints have of course always more or less deliberately undergone such training. The characteristic of the present age is not only urgent need for such training, but the readiness for it of larger numbers than hitherto. We have mentioned the masses as winning a share in sovereignty, in the wake of the middle classes and the aristocracies. The masses have done so only, of course, by attaining to the self-consciousness hitherto possessed by the few in power. The experience of some clergy alive to these issues suggests that, just as the previously merely conscious masses have inherited the self-consciousness of the few, so a greater number than hitherto of the self-conscious are now ready to seek the all-consciousness which the sages, mystics and saints in some degree possess.

Some may agree that readiness for some measure of all-consciousness is more widespread today than hitherto, but strongly disagree with the publication of what amounts to an excercise in embodying The Infinite. Those who are ready for such training may be trusted to find it privately, as always hitherto. To publish even its elementary stages exposes it to misunderstanding and possibly to misuse, and thereby exposes the very cause it is meant to serve to untold harm.

This is certainly the traditional view, and we give it due weight. Nevertheless, we regard the crisis of our time as so urgent, and man in danger of inflicting such fearful suffering on himself, that it is necessary to modify this tradition. Furthermore, we believe that many more people are capable of such training than are fully aware of it. Hence they not only suffer more or less acute frustration, but their potential capacity is wasted. The size of the next step towards ultimate human self-fulfilment depends upon the use they are helped to make of their dormant capacity. They will probably otherwise abuse it and greatly add to the danger of the crisis.

But even so it is necessary to safeguard the subject from misunderstanding or misuse by making clear for whom this book is intended. In the first place of course it is intended for those who have read so far without essential disagreement. In the second place, and more importantly, it is intended for those who are prepared to act on what they have read, not as a leisure occupation, but as their most important work, no matter how they earn their living. This no doubt primarily means those who are in Holy Orders or in some form of the Ministry by genuine *vocation*. They appreciate something of the enormous privilege their vocation offers them, and gladly accept the corresponding responsibility of spiritual leadership this lays upon them. Here hierarchical rank is totally irrelevant. Realising that no other form of leadership calls for more complete self-effacement, they understand that no other work on earth can discipline and fit a man more directly to incarnate The Infinite.[1]

But this book is not intended only for those in Holy Orders or the Ministry. If it is to serve the synthesis of the three chief approaches to the Reality, it must have some relevance for all who consciously seek the highest degree of the Reality, for all who consciously seek ultimate self-fulfilment, in whatever terms they conceive this two-sided purpose. For all such are in some degree at least potentially part of the "priesthood of all believers", that is to say believers in the infinite Reality and in man's illimitable destiny. Whether they regard themselves as members of religious bodies, as secularists, or as humanists is not primarily relevant. What determines their

[1] Heb. 12,10.

23

rank in this universal priesthood is the degree of their dedication in seeking the infinite Reality.

It only remains for us to indicate what is meant here by dedication to these ends. For this may be understood in quite trivial analogical senses. We understand it in the exact sense, and it becomes clear only in the light of man's ultimate destiny. If corporeal selves are to express the Goodness, Beauty and Truth of The Spiritual SELF, and through Him the Glory of The Infinite, it is obvious that they must learn to be in corporeal terms as He is in spiritual terms.[1] They must learn to think, feel and act in space and time according to His eternal pattern, if they are to unfold the corporeal Reality from the spiritual Reality, and from the infinite Reality beyond all. In the first place, therefore, dedication means submission to the most far-reaching process of learning that is conceivable. It means discarding all such partial truths as are perceived from the religious, secular and humanist standpoints *in isolation*, however painfully they have been gained, and learn from The Supreme SELF Who is The Truth.[2]

Now His unitive, universal, spiritual thinking, feeling and activity cannot be the natural corporeal self's merely writ large, even supremely large. The reason for this will become plain in later chapters. Here we need only mention that if the corporeal is a manifold and diverse representation of that which is spiritually unitive and universal, the difference must be one of kind and not merely of degree. The difference has been well expressed in the following epigram. "Things are because The SELF knows them; selves know things because they are." The Bible records The SELF as expressly declaring this difference. "MY Thoughts are not your thoughts, neither are your ways MY Ways".[3] The difference must be that between the remotest opposites. The process of learning from The SELF Who is the all-inclusive Truth thus involves a complete transformation of all partitive thinking, feeling and activity which pertain to the natural corporeal self.[4]

The transformation begins with *purgation* from such thinking, feeling and activity. If these are the diametrical opposite of that

[1] 1 Jn. 4,17.
[2] Mat. 11,29; Jn. 14,6.
[3] Isa. 55,8.
[4] Rom. 12,2.

which they must become, there can be no compromise with them. They must be "put off" so completely that the process is described as the death, crucifixion, annihilation of the entire natural self.[1] This is not, of course, the annihilation of selfhood, as is sometimes erroneously supposed. Otherwise The SELF could not be "put on".[2] The annihilation is that of the *partitive* thinking, feeling and activity of the natural self which prevents the *integral* all-inclusive Mind, Heart and Will of The SELF being expressed in corporeal terms.

As the natural corporeal self is purged, it is able to receive the *illumination* or enlightenment of the Mind, Heart and Will of The SELF, and thereby to "put on" The SELF. Illumination is thus not confined to the mind, with which alone knowledge is usually associated, but embraces also the whole feeling and active facets of the self. Now if this process of complete enlightenment or illumination is regarded conversely, it is of course the progressive incarnation of the Mind, Heart and Will of The SELF in the corporeal self. Corresponding changes are thereby caused in the natural corporeal self, and they are so radical as to merit being called its resurrection from mortality to immortality.

Since the illumination of the purged natural self and the progressive incarnation in it of The SELF are but opposite aspects of the same process, this is consummated in the at-onement or *union* of the two extremes of personality. This union may be described as the point where ascent and descent converge in the perfect incarnation of The SELF in the self. At this point the self knows The SELF to be its own True Self, which then expresses in trans-figured corporeal terms the Goodness, Beauty and Truth of The SELF, and through Him the Glory of The Infinite.[3]

This book is intended for those who are prepared to face, not only the purgation of their natural self, but the immensely greater effort of submitting to its illumination by The SELF. They alone can hope to attain, and sustain, union with The SELF wherein the purpose of their existence is fulfilled.

---

[1] Gal. 2,20; Eph. 4,22.
[2] Gal. 3,27.
[3] Jn. 1,14.

Chapter 2

The ONE

[1]

The reader has now been introduced to the whole scope of this book. Part I outlines our view of the Reality, which we have seen to be threefold. Part II suggests a way, found to be practicable in the present age, of attempting to embody the Reality in its supreme degree, to unfold it in corporeal terms, and thereby to express its Glory, which is the ultimate purpose of human existence.

The preface mentions the origin of this book and states that it springs from spiritual experience. Strictly, therefore, Part I should open with some description of such experience, before going on to deal with its rationalisation as a scheme of the Reality. It would be of dubious value to describe our own experience of the indwelling presence of The Supreme SELF. Such experience can only be indicated in terms of imagery, analogy, symbolism, and any terms we might use may mean little to others. We propose therefore to open Part I by using a single fairly well-known symbol which is found in some variant in most of the great religious traditions. It is generally regarded as extremely ancient, though its significance is seldom clearly understood, or properly valued. We should beware of regarding this symbol as primitive, in the sense of elementary, because of its antiquity or lack of being appreciated. If it is primitive, it is so in the sense of primary, essential, fontal. Its simplicity is that of hidden and not yet unfolded depth. It is the most universal representation we have found of the deepest human experience of the indwelling presence of The Supreme SELF.

This symbol has many advantages, the most important being its simple, clearcut, abstract nature, which gives it the accuracy of a geometrical figure. It thus provides us not only with a most reliable representation of the experience to be rationalised as our scheme of the Reality, but with the most accurate starting point for the rationalisation itself, the point from which we can most safely unfold it. Our own experience will be touched on in the course of setting out the exercises in Part II, when it will be seen to accord with the experience represented by the symbol. This should be some measure of the universality of our own experience.

Let us begin with a short description of the symbol. We have chosen the variant which appears to us as most comprehensive and suited to our purpose. It consists of a circle containing two interlaced triangles, one upright and the other inverted, and the whole is surrounded by twelve rays. The symbol is shown on the flyleaf, and should be constantly referred to as we expound its significance, in so far as we have grasped it, and as we fill in our outline with as much detail as the exercises in Part II call for. We do not propose to include in our scheme of the Reality any more detail than can be applied in practical life. What does the symbol signify?

We will base our exposition upon a statement summarising the Reality, in so far as such a thing is possible, and then correlate it with the symbol. This statement is also of great antiquity, and may be regarded as no less profound and universal than the symbol. The two put together represent the most profound insight into the Reality, based on experience, which is known to us. This complementary statement is to be found in an ancient tradition called the Chaldean Oracle. According to this, the Reality is threefold, its three aspects or degrees being called The ONE, The THREE and The MANY. We shall presently quote the statement more fully, but for the moment need no more than the above.

We now turn to correlate the symbol with this extract from the Chaldean Oracle, and use the latter to expound the former. This will give us the starting point, the kernel from which to unfold our own exposition. We shall do so in three successive stages, according to the three aspects or degrees of the Reality, thus following its own unfoldment from hidden simplicity to manifested and expressed complexity, as though filling in a comprehensive but blank outline with increasing detail. This should safeguard our unfoldment from over or underrating any of its details at the expense of the whole, and thus from distortion. For, as just mentioned, we shall be trying to follow the progressive expression of the Reality as it is projected in manifestation from its supreme hidden source.

[2]

Having suggested the method we propose to follow in unfolding our view of the Reality, let us now briefly consider the symbol as interpreted by the oracle. Space allows us no more than an impressionist view.

Essentially the symbol is an all-inclusive circle which encloses two equal triangles interlaced and which is surrounded by twelve rays. These three components, together giving off the rays, are distinct from each other, yet so interrelated that they form a perfect whole. If any change is made by removing or displacing any component, the perfect symmetry of the whole is lost. We may take this all-inclusive circle to signify the entire threefold Reality, in the glory of its absolute, eternal, infinite wholeness. It is perfect from all conceivable points of view and in all conceivable senses. The oracle designates the threefold Reality as the wholeness of The ONE, The THREE and The MANY.

We next consider each of these three components of the symbol separately. We begin with the circle. It is the greatest of the components, is complete and perfect in its circularity, is without the limitations of beginning and ending, and itself appears a simple blank. We may take this to signify the Reality in its primal aspect as undifferentiated unity, the Reality in its supreme degree of absolute, eternal, infinite. Though the circle exceeds the two triangles it contains, it touches them at all points, yet remains distinct from all. This signifies that, although the infinite Reality transcends all, it includes all and is immanent in all, yet itself remains exempt from all in its primal wholeness and perfection. The circle is clearly that which the oracle calls The ONE.

We now consider the two triangles within the circle. The upright one is the more familiar geometrical figure and is the first to claim attention, overshadowing the inverted one. We may take this to signify the degree of the Reality next to the infinite in eminence, universality and power. This is the spiritual aspect or degree. The triangle contains three angles, and thus clearly corresponds with The THREE mentioned by the oracle. Yet these three angles are integrated in the triangle to form a whole. This signifies that The THREE must essentially be understood as triune. We shall therefore henceforward speak of The Triunity except when actually quoting the oracle, and always understand The THREE in this way.

Lastly we come to the inverted triangle. It is the inverted counterpart or image of the upright one and is overshadowed by its original. We take the inverted triangle to signify the degree of the Reality which is least eminent, universal and potent. This least, most particularised, and most limited degree is the corporeal. We note however that in its totality it corresponds with the spiritual. The inverted triangle can only be that which the oracle calls The MANY. It may however be asked in what sense a single triangle represents manyness. Alone it certainly does not do so. But when it is placed upon the upright one as the latter's reflection, image, counterpart, it immediately gives rise to six smaller triangles. They may be said to come forth from the single inverted one in its act of reflecting its upright original. Yet the six all remain rooted in their single source. At the same time they form a complex whole with it. The inverted triangle thus has three aspects: that of a single prototype, of its many derivations, and of their integration in a richer unity. We have seen that a triangle signifies triunity. We may therefore take the inverted triangle to signify corporeal triunity as single-multiple-corporate. As such it may be quite correctly called The MANY.

It remains for us to touch on the twelve rays. They surround the complete symbol with a symmetry which matches its own. Being outside the all-containing circle, they cannot signify yet another degree of the Reality. For there is nothing outside it. We may take them to signify the glory which shines forth from the fully unfolded Reality as a whole. The fact that they are considered last of all implies that the threefold Whole alone is all-glorious.

Having considered the three chief components of the symbol, we may see it as a whole once more with greater understanding. It represents the entire Reality in its three great aspects or degrees of Unity, Triunity, and one-many-corporate Triunity. Yet though these three aspects are distinct, they are all interrelated to form one great Whole. The circle touches the triangles which it includes and keeps them both indissolubly interlaced, so that one exactly reflects the other. Thus forming a six-pointed star enclosed in a circle and surrounded by twelve rays, the whole remains exactly the same whatever angle it is viewed from. The whole Reality, threefold as infinite, spiritual and corporeal, is changeless. For

29

whatever change there is in it is unceasing and therefore itself changeless.

This view of the whole Reality as changelessly including all change is the primary one. From the infinite standpoint, if the all-inclusive may be called a point, the Reality must appear static in its eternally abiding perfection. But this view is wholly beyond the natural human understanding subject to change, and means little. In dealing with what eternally *is,* it does not reveal what everlastingly *happens.* To discover this, we must study the symbol, and the threefold Reality it signifies, in the dynamic terms of process. For this we again turn to the Chaldean Oracle and now consider the actual text therein which is concerned with our subject. It begins as follows: "The ONE spake, and immediately The THREE came forth and became The MANY".[1] We return to the symbol in the light of this text.

As before, we begin with the all-inclusive component, the circle. Since we are now concerned with what *happens* rather than *is,* we begin by seeing the circle as blank. The blank circle signifies The ONE before making any utterance. Therefore nothing has yet proceeded from The ONE, and neither of the triangles are manifested, still being unexpressed in the infinite profundity of The ONE. But now The ONE speaks; and immediately The THREE come forth. So the upright triangle appears within the circle. Here we find the very first manifestation, expression, unfoldment of the hidden Unity into Triunity.

We see that the upright triangle fits precisely within the circle. This signifies that though The Triunity is less than The Unity in one sense, this is not so in another. The Triunity is less than The Unity in the sense that no expression can be exactly equal with the expressor; otherwise there would be no distinction between them. In the other sense The Triunity *is* The Unity as the latter first stands forth spiritually manifested. The Triunity *is* the infinite Unity in spiritual terms.

The oracle goes on to state that in coming forth from The ONE, The THREE immediately become The MANY. As we have seen,

---

[1] The text is available to us only in an English translation. There are no doubt other versions and probably translations into other languages. If they differed more than superficially, they would destroy the significance of the original.

The MANY are signified by the inverted triangle. As soon as the upright triangle appears within the circle, the inverted one does so too as its image, reflection, counterpart, when both inseparably interlaced form the symmetry of the six-pointed star. The manifestation of the infinite Unity as the spiritual Triunity is thus immediately reflected in a corresponding and inseparable manifestation of its counterpart, the corporeal Triunity. And this, as we have seen, has three aspects: that of a single prototypal one, of a multitude, and of their integration in a corporate and therefore richer oneness.

When viewed dynamically, the symbol thus represents the threefold Reality as a process of The Infinite's self-manifestation, self-expression, self-unfoldment, first in spiritual, and then immediately in corporeal terms. This procession may equally well be described as The Infinite's self-projection out of hidden Unity into spiritual Triunity and into the one-many-oneness of corporeal Triunity. It is of course possible to attribute selfhood, process, procession, etc. to The Infinite only analogically. These analogies are the simplest way to indicate what *happens* instantly yet ceaselessly.

The dynamic view of the threefold Reality has amplified the primary changeless view. But we need a further amplification if the purpose of the process is to be clear. Having seen what ceaselessly happens, let us once more consider the symbol in order to see *why* it happens. We may call this the ideal view of the Reality, the view in terms of purpose and fulfilment.

We turn again to the oracle to interpret the symbol in these ideal terms. Having stated that The ONE spake and immediately The THREE came forth and became The MANY, the text goes on to describe the sequel. "The MANY returned again through The THREE into The ONE." The ultimate reason *why* The ONE proceeds through The THREE into The MANY must therefore lie in some purpose that is fulfilled by the return of The MANY into The THREE and of The THREE into The ONE. We resume the study of the symbol in order to discover this purpose.

Since we are now concerned with the return of The MANY, we must obviously study the symbol in the reverse order of before. We must begin with the inverted triangle and trace its return, first into the upright one, and finally into the circle. At first sight the significance of this reverse view of the symbol seems too obvious for comment. The one-many-corporate Triunity becomes reunited with its Spiritual Original of which it is the counterpart, and through this with The Unity which is the source of all. But a little reflection will suggest that there must be a deeper significance in the return than the mere restoration of the original situation. If the circle were left blank in the end as it was in the beginning, the procession from and return into Unity would have no intelligible purpose. These movements would be an expansion and contraction, an ebb and flow, which accomplished nothing. What does the return of The MANY then really signify?

The general significance of the symbol points to the answer. The symbol, let us remember, signifies the whole threefold Reality fully unfolded. Therefore, as soon as the two triangles have appeared in the circle, they may not be deleted without destroying the significance of the symbol. If they were deleted, it would cease to signify the entire unfolded Reality. The real significance of the return of The MANY into The THREE, and through The THREE into The ONE, must therefore be sought in a combination of their return into Unity without ceasing to be Multitude. They must in some manner return into the unique Triunity and through this into the supreme Unity, without a single one of them losing its identity.

How is such a combination, such a synthesis, arrived at? We reach it if *each* of The MANY remains outwardly separate but becomes inwardly united with The THREE, and through The THREE with The ONE. So *each* of the many Triunities becomes a uniquely particular outward expression of the universal Triunity which is inwardly present in them all, and thereby an expression of the ineffable Unity beyond all. Now The MANY, being thus inwardly united with each other through The THREE, must become related with one another outwardly also. Their inward unity binds them into a corporate body. But since they do not thereby cease to be The MANY, the individuality of each is preserved intact in this body. Then the many Triunities individually and collectively express in outward terms that which the universal Triunity is in inward terms, and through the latter that which the Unity is beyond all.

The MANY can express The ONE in no other way. *Each* of them expresses The THREE, and *together* they express The

ONE. So individually *and* collectively The MANY represent in outward corporeal terms that which The THREE represents in inward spiritual terms, and that which The ONE ineffably *is* beyond all. This is the purpose of their existence, and its fulfilment generates the twelve rays which signify the glory of the whole threefold Reality fully unfolded.

This may also be stated conversely, in order still further to clarify it. The ONE, through The THREE, proceeds into and returns from The MANY, in order through them to manifest the glory of the infinite Reality in corporeal terms. So the infinite Reality, revealed in *each* of The MANY and *all* of The MANY *together*, and thereby as fully revealed as is possible, manifestly shines forth in glory.

Such is the reason, then, why The ONE proceeds from and returns into "His" ineffable Unity. Now such a procession, fulfilled in the course of its return, may suggest a final end. If so, this would imply a limitation of Infinity. It may therefore be necessary once more to consider the symbol and try to see its significance as free of limits as possible. Space allows us only to mention the most important and possibly the most obvious points. (In a sense, of course, there is no limit to the limitations that could erroneously be imposed on Infinity).

The first point to note is that the processions and returns of The ONE can never cease, can have no limit in number, can never repeat themselves. Hence The MANY can never cease to come forth, can have no limit in number, can never be alike. There can no more be repetition in the course of The ONE's manifestation of Infinity than each return is a repetition of each procession. We must therefore understand the endless processions and returns of The ONE to continue endlessly, generating an endlessly diverse quantity of The MANY. For only a quantitative endlessness can express Infinity in the corporeal terms of space, time and change, in so far as this is possible.

The next point to note is that the endless cycles of The ONE's procession and return, generating the endlessly MANY, can never produce a repetition in their results. We must therefore understand the cycles to lead to an endlessly increasing degree of fulfilment, generating The MANY in endlessly increasing quality. For only a qualitative endlessness can express Infinity in the corporeal terms of space, time and change, in so far as this is possible.

We can mention only one more point in trying to remove limitations from our view of Infinity. We have just seen that The ONE manifests "His" Infinity in corporeal terms in cycles of fulfilment which are endless in quantity and quality, and which endlessly grow therein. We must now understand that in the last analysis all that can be said in trying to break free of limitations is valid only analogically. For The ONE is beyond procession and return, and therefore beyond fulfilment. Although including all things, The ONE wholly transcends them. The ONE's absolute, eternal, infinite Reality is in the last analysis never less than perfectly manifested, expressed, unfolded. But that is so to The ONE alone, and to none else.

[3]

Having considered the symbol as interpreted by the text we have chosen from the Chaldean Oracle, we now have to unfold our scheme of the Reality from this basis, the most universal we have found. Its simple, clearcut abstract nature should minimise the risk of distorting our unfoldment in the course of making it.

Since this book is primarily, though not of course exclusively, addressed to Europeans, that is heirs of the Christian tradition, our scheme will be set out in Christian theological terms, wherever necessary supported by philosophy and science. As the preface made clear, however, technical language will be reduced to the minimum. Wherever possible biblical terms will be used, and these will be understood in the sense of mystical rather than of other branches of theology. For as experience has shown us, these are the terms which are most intelligible to people of other religions, and often to people who do not profess any. The mystical must therefore be the most universal sense of these terms. Heirs of other traditions can, if they choose, work out the scheme in their own terms. If our scheme is sound, the same can be done, though probably at much greater length, in terms of any philosophy, science or art required for secular or specifically humanist purposes.

We should face, from the start, one of the biggest difficulties in stating the theological view we are about to set out. The same difficulty is bound to face whoever tries to understand it. This

34

difficulty springs from the fact that the Reality, being threefold, can equally truly be viewed from three distinct points of view. (There are many others, of course, but they are derived from these three basic ones.) These are the changeless, the dynamic and the ideal standpoints of The ONE, The THREE and The MANY respectively. Owing to these distinctions between them, these standpoints may sometimes appear contradictory, until we awaken to the all-inclusive standpoint of The ONE as it unfolds within us. Patience and forebearance will be needed in studying what follows, especially in the extremely compressed form demanded by a book which aims at practice as well as theory. The subject is bound to be as hard to grasp as it has been to set out in such a compressed form.

As we have already seen, we can say least about the standpoint of The ONE because it includes most, and the rest of this chapter will have to suffice for its expanded statement in Christian terms. The dynamic standpoint of The THREE and the ideal one of The MANY will need more space, and each therefore has a chapter to itself. We return then to the symbol and fix our attention on the circle which contains the two interlaced triangles. For the time being we omit the twelve surrounding rays. As we have seen, the all-inclusive circle signifies The ONE, the absolute, eternal, infinite Reality which transcends all, is immanent in all, yet is exempt from all it pervades and contains. We identify this with God Who is above all, through all, and in all.[1] This is God in ineffable fullness, eternally changeless, absolutely and yet infinitely perfect.[2] God transcends all process and fulfilment, yet comprehends them.[3] To God the spiritual and corporeal aspects of the Reality, signified by the two triangles, are fully present and expressed. But to God alone. God fills Heaven and Earth, that is to say, the spiritual and corporeal realms.[4]

Since God is above *all*, God is above being. And therefore above egoity, personality, selfhood. And therefore beyond knowledge, imagination, conception.[5] Hence nothing can strictly be said

---

[1] Eph. 4,6.
[2] Eph. 1,23; Mal. 3,6; Mat. 5,48.
[3] Acts 17,28; Col. 1,17 RV.
[4] Jer. 23,24.
[5] 1 Cor. 2,11.

of God in "His" unknowable fulness except in an endless series of self-cancelling paradoxes. A few are given by way of illustration. God is above being and "is" not, yet undoubtedly *is*. But God also neither *is* nor is not. God is IT, yet HE. But God also is neither IT nor HE. God is unknowable, yet knowable. But God is also neither unknowable nor knowable. And so on ad infinitum with decreasing meaning. For God transcends yet comprehends all opposites, as well as their reconciliations. There is no purpose in trying to say anything of God in "His" fulness, except as a help in breaking through the limitations of rational thought into the realm of devotion, which is beyond reason while including reason. We have tried to say it only because it is supremely important to break through these limitations.

We turn next to the upright triangle which signifies The **THREE**, the unique Triunity. We have seen that this represents the Reality as it is first of all unfolded from Unity in spiritual terms, the Reality in its spiritual degree or aspect. It is thus the fontal, archetypal, universal aspect of all that is contained in God, in so far as it can be known. We may call this the whole knowable Reality in its spiritual degree or aspect. Or, since spiritual things can only be spiritually known, we may call this the entire field of spiritual knowledge.[1]

Let us now consider the entire field of knowledge, spiritual or otherwise, at present open to man. If we begin our review from the a priori standpoint, we may suppose the field to consist of three great areas. If we then review it as it has been won by man, we shall find that human experience bears out our supposition. On these grounds we must suppose the first area of human knowledge to be concerned with whatever man regards as God. But, as we have stated, God is unknowable. Yet some aspect of God must be knowable, otherwise there would be no religious experience. And experience in some form of the supreme Source, Creator, Author, or whatever name man gives to God, seems to be the earliest factor that has guided human life. We may therefore take the first great area of human knowledge to be concerned with God, in so far as God is knowable.

The second area is implied by the first. Authorship implies

[1] 1. Cor. 2,14.

36

operations, works. The second area of human knowledge may therefore be supposed to be concerned with God's works. History appears to bear this out. For having begun by more or less indiscriminately seeing God in all things about him, man has learned to distinguish creation from the Creator. We may therefore take the second great area of knowledge to be concerned with the Universe, in its widest sense as the field of God's operations and the record of God's works.

The second area implies the third. All intelligent work must have some purpose, the attainment of which is its fulfilment. We should therefore suppose the third area of knowledge to be concerned with the fulfilment of God's creative operations. We should expect it to be concerned with the opus achieved by God's operations, the work which is the fulfilment of God's works. The nature of this fulfilment of God's works is indicated by the third great area of knowledge to be won by man. Having become conscious of the Universe he inhabits, man begins by regarding himself as part of it. But as his consciousness grows, he discovers himself to be distinct from the Universe. In fact, he becomes self-conscious, and realises that though *in* the Universe he is not *of* it. We therefore take the third great area of human knowledge to be concerned with Man, in the widest sense as the fulfilled work of God and lord of the Universe.

Let us then assume that everything humanly knowable must be some aspect of the knowable *God* as Author of all, of the *Universe* as the works of God, and of *Man* as the fulfilled work of God, as the fulfilment of God's works. Now if this represents the knowable Reality which man has discovered and is penetrating into ever more deeply, it is obvious that the Reality existed prior to its discovery. And it must subsist in its spiritual aspect before its corporeal one. The significance of the upright triangle in the symbol we are considering should now become clear. As we have seen, it represents the whole knowable Reality in its spiritual aspect. Each of its angles may therefore be taken to signify one of the three great features of the spiritual Reality.

The angle at the apex of the triangle, being above the others, signifies God, in so far as God is knowable. Moving clockwise to the lower angle on the right, we take this to signify the works of God in their spiritual aspect, the Spiritual Universe. The lower angle on the left then signifies the fulfilment of God's spiritual works, Spiritual Man.

In discussing these three features as areas of knowledge, we have seen them to be distinct but closely related. The fact that they are signified by three angles of a triangle suggests that they are so closely related as to form a triunity. We may therefore take it that the spiritual Reality, that is, the knowable God, Spiritual Universe and Spiritual Man, is a single indissoluble triunity. We must now suggest how these three great features of the spiritual Reality may be understood as a triunity in Christian terms.

The first feature is the knowable God, of Whom we shall say no more for the moment. We next consider the Spiritual Universe as the works of God the supreme Author. Now essentially an author's works are the activity by which consciously or unconsciously he reveals himself. And the more truly creative the author is, the more his works represent the projection of *himself*. Essentially, therefore, the Spiritual Universe represents the field of God's operations and the record of His works in the process of His spiritual revelation of Himself. Hence the Bible speaks of the Heavens (the spiritual realm) as declaring the Glory of God.[1] Finally we consider Man. We have stated man to be the fulfilment of God's works, God's magnum opus. Now one may say that an author's works are truly fulfilled in the degree that his resulting opus faithfully reveals all that he seeks to express. And this is ultimately himself. This points us to the significance of Spiritual Man as the fulfilled opus of God. Spiritual Man is the spiritually expressed projection of God, the spiritual image of God. Spiritual Man is The SELF Who expresses the super-selfhood of God Who is above personality.

If we put these three features of the spiritual Reality together into a triunity, we see Spiritual Man as the total all-comprehending utterance, in spiritual terms, of the unknowable God. For He sums up the triunity of the knowable God, His works the Spiritual Universe, and their fulfilment Spiritual Man. In that sense He is its Lord, the Lord from and of Heaven, as S. Paul calls Him.[2] He *is*, in fact, the whole knowable Reality in its spiritual aspect. He *is* the spiritual Reality. Hence the Bible calls Him the Son, Image,

[1] Ps. 19,1.
[2] 1 Cor. 15,47 AV & RV.

Word of God.[1] But He most significantly calls Himself I AM and declares that this is His Name for ever.[2]

It remains for us to consider the inverted triangle and set out its significance in Christian terms. Since this triangle with its smaller subsidiaries signifies The MANY, that is, the one-many-corporate Triunity, our exposition will take a little longer in this case. For this triangle signifies the whole knowable Reality in its corporeal aspect, the Reality as it is corporeally knowable, the Reality as it is unfolded to its outermost and most complex conditions of space, time and change. It will be as well to recall the composition of this one-many-corporate Triunity which symbolises the endless multitude and variety of the corporeal realm, whose complexity nevertheless forms a triune whole. This Triunity consists first of a single prototypal one, then of the multitude it gives rise to, and lastly of the reunion of the multitude into a corporate body in which the individuality of each member is preserved.

Let us begin by noting that the inverted triangle is an exact inversion of the upright one, and that the two are interlaced. This means that the one-many-corporate Triunity, which is the corporeal Reality, is an inseparable inversion of the archetypal Triunity which is the spiritual Reality. Since we have seen the latter to be The SELF, I AM, we can indicate the meaning of the inversion. It signifies the relationship between subjectivity and objectivity. The corporeal Reality is the indispensable objective counterpart of the spiritual. But what does this mean? We know that the spiritual Reality is The Word comprising the knowable God, Spiritual Universe and Spiritual Man Who is The SELF, I AM. How are these three features represented in their counterpart, the corporeal Reality?

We must begin by considering the corporeal Reality in its single prototypal aspect, before going on to its manyness and reconstituted corporate wholeness. The first and most important question to answer is: how can the knowable God be represented in the corporeal Reality? Since God is Spirit, the only possible answer is: by His Spirit. God's works, the Spiritual Universe, must then be represented by His Spirit's works, the Corporeal Universe. And God's fulfilled opus, Spiritual Man, I AM, must be represented

[1] Jn. 3,18; Col. 1,15; Jn. 1,1.
[2] Ex. 3,14 & 15.

by His Spirit's fulfilled work, Corporeal Man. Which is how the Bible, in its own terms, envisages God's presence, activity and incarnation on earth.[1]

Corporeal Man must therefore be also I AM. To distinguish Him from His spiritual archetype, we might designate Him as *I AM*. But since He is the inseparable objective counterpart of His subjective SELF, His ME vis-a-vis His I, we ought then to designate Him as I AM — *I AM*. This is too clumsy, and so we shall speak of Him as I AM or The SELF and only use the italicised form when the distinction specially requires to be brought out. For *I AM* is I AM in so far as the latter is knowable in the corporeal realm, rather as the earthward side of the sun alone is visible on the earth. This is He Whom the Bible calls The Christ, and Who is elsewhere sometimes called the Cosmic Christ in distinction from His presence in Jesus. Since He corporeally represents The Word, Who spiritually represents God, His full title should perhaps be God-Word-Christ. But as this is impossibly clumsy, we shall speak of Him as The Word or The Christ. Whenever practicable, however, we shall speak of Him as I AM or The SELF. For I AM is His truest name, indeed His only absolutely correct name, and by which He therefore calls Himself. To call Him by any other name is to attach an objective label to Him Who is the supreme Subject, The SELF, I AM.

We next pass on to the corporeal Reality in its manifold aspect. How can the spiritual Triunity of the knowable God, Spiritual Universe and Spiritual Man Who is The Word, The SELF, I AM, be represented in each of the endless multitude and diversity of corporeal Triunities? I AM can only be represented in each on the same principle as He is in their single prototype, The Christ. For all are essentially the manifold and diverse aspects of The Christ. Thus all must share in His Holy Spirit Who is God in them. All must share in His works manifested as the Corporeal Universe, their particular share being their personal body and environment. And all must share in the fulfilment of His works, which is the perfect manhood of each. All are thus triunities, and as such particularised objective counterparts of The Word: Christed men, Selves, I ams. The corporeal human triunity is more familiar as that of Spirit, Soul and Body, but these terms

[1] E.g. Ezek. 39,29; 1 Cor. 12,4; Jn. 1,14:

have the same defect as "The Word" or "The Christ" in making *things* of what are essentially aspects of selfhood, and we shall avoid them whenever possible. These Selves, I ams, are they whom the Bible calls the Saints in Light.[1] Their perfect type is Jesus, Who is therefore Christ. Hence He calls them His brethren.[2] For He is *with them* conterminous with The Christ.

This brings us to the third aspect of the corporeal Reality. This aspect consists of the endless multitude and diversity of corporeal triunities just mentioned, reconstituted in a corporate unity, a wholeness, a body in which the individuality of each member is preserved intact. Only such an endless multitude and diversity of triunities, united throughout all worlds and ages and embracing all conditions, can be the complete objective counterpart of the universal spiritual Triunity and thus fully represent the latter in the outermost corporeal conditions of space, time and change. *Each,* being fully aware of the Holy Spirit of God within, is thereby inwardly united with all others. So by the Holy Spirit all *together* represent God in terms of space, time and change. Each, since he is moved by the Holy Spirit, works in harmony with all others. The fulfilment of the harmonious work is perfect Corporate Man, the perfect Human Society, throughout the whole realm of space, time and change. This is that which the Bible calls the Body of Christ, the Holy Church, the Temple of God.[3]

This Society, being the complete objective counterpart of The SELF, through Him thus represents the total Word of God unfolded in corporeal terms. Each member is *a* word of the total Utterance; yet the total Utterance is fully present in each. This Society, fully embodying The SELF, through Him represents God in the flesh throughout all worlds, all ages and all conditions. The individual bodies of the members of this Society become transfigured by the presence of God incarnate in them.[4] And so the corporate Body, including its environment extending throughout all space, time and change, becomes transfigured. It shines forth as a jewelled corona of Goodness, Beauty and Truth.[5] This is the Glory of God which

---

[1] Col. 1,12.
[2] Heb. 2,11.
[3] Eph. 4,12; Col. 1,18; 2 Cor. 6,16.
[4] Mk. 9,2.
[5] Mal. 3,17; Mat. 13,43.

fills Heaven and Earth.[1] It is signified by the twelve rays which surround the symbol. This is the Glory of the infinite Reality fully manifested, expressed, unfolded in *both* spiritual and corporeal terms. So it ever was, is, and will be from the changeless, infinitely perfect standpoint of The Holy One, and all the Holy Ones who share therein.

[1] Tersanctus.

Chapter 3

The THREE: The SELF

[1]

The previous chapter showed the threefold Reality from the
eternally changeless, all-transcending, all-containing standpoint of
The ONE, God the Holy One. In this light the Reality in its
three degrees of infinite, spiritual and corporeal may be regarded
as the three chief aspects of God. The infinite is hidden in super-
essential, super-personal, super-intelligible Unity. All that ever was,
is, will, or could be manifested is nevertheless fully unfolded to
God. Of course. But to God alone. God first manifests the
infinite Reality in spiritual terms. This spiritual image or expression
of God is The Word, I AM, The SELF. And through Him God
immediately manifests His objective counterpart, the Reality in
corporeal terms. This corporeal image or expression is the one-
many-corporate Christ, *I AM, The SELF.* So by dwelling and
working in individual and corporate Christed *Selves* God builds
"His" Holy Temple on earth after the pattern of the heavenly,
and the Glory of "His" infinite Reality is manifested in the outermost corporeal conditions of space, time and change.[1]

In the present chapter we shall try to show the threefold Reality
from the dynamic standpoint of The THREE, The Word, The
SELF, I AM. We shall first trace His procession from the hidden
Unity of God into spiritual manifestation, in the course of which
He creates its corporeal counterpart. And then we shall trace His
gathering-together of the endless multitude and diversity of His
Creation, in the course of which He comes to dwell and work in
corporeal Selves.[2] But though this standpoint, being dynamic implies
process, this is purely spiritual and involves no space and time,
even though it partly takes place therein. For as God transcends

[1] 2 Cor. 6,16; Eph. 2,21; Ex. 25,9 RV.
[2] Jn. 11,52; Eph. 1,10.

43

The SELF even while immanent in Him, so The SELF transcends all selves even while dwelling and working in them.

We shall unfold this standpoint on the same pattern as before, starting with the simplest outline and filling this in with detail in clear-cut stages. We shall thus first consider *what* The SELF does everlastingly (the static view), then *how* He does all things (the dynamic view), and finally *why* He does them (the ideal view). It is necessary to remember that, if nothing can properly be said of God, nothing can properly *not* be said of the Word of God. For He, The SELF, is all that is knowable. Whatever detail we put into our outline will therefore itself be the result of ruthless pruning.

We begin at the point at which The SELF is begotten, the point at which I AM comes forth from God's all-transcending hidden Unity.[1] Glancing back at the symbol, we here see the upright triangle first appear within the hitherto blank circle. This is the point at which the infinite Reality, hidden in the cloud of absolute unknowing, first becomes spiritually knowable. (One may illustrate this with the sun, hidden beyond the horizon, projecting its first flash of light). As God first makes "Himself" knowable, "He" stands forth as personal. (Having used inverted commas to stress that up to this point God is super-personal, this clumsy device should not be further necessary). God makes Himself knowable as I AM, as the first flash of light reveals the sun above the horizon. As we have seen, I AM is the eternal Name of God, the truest Name of the Unnameable One. This is the Name above every name, to be remembered for ever.[2] For it is the essence of all selfhood. "I AM", He declares, "This is MY memorial unto all generations".[3]

The revelation of God as I AM immediately implies Being. For I AM *is*, or more grammatically, I AM. Since Being is in the highest degree personal, it is supremely alive. And for the same reason Living Being is supremely intelligent or knowing. Ultimately I AM is *the* all-inclusive Knowing, Living Being. "I AM", He declares, "the Living One".[4] But since as yet we see Him only spiritually manifested, here He is more properly described by the

---

[1] Jn. 16, 28.
[2] Phil. 2,9.
[3] Ex. 3,15.
[4] Rev. 1,18 RV.

44

universal term of Knowing, Living Being or Essence.

Now Knowing, Living Being implies spiritual activity. In revealing Himself as I AM, He also thereby produces the sphere of His activity. This explains the sense in which the previous chapter mentions His operations or works as constituting the spiritual realm or Universe. We also saw there that the fulfilment of His works, the complete opus, is the lord of the spiritual realm, Spiritual Man. This reference to lordship indicates the sense in which these works are fulfilled. They are fulfilled by being crowned with complete accomplishment, wherein the perfect spiritual image or expression of God stands revealed as The Word, The SELF. This is the crowned lord of God's works. This is I AM clothed in the Spiritual Universe and in that sense "embodied" in it; its fulfilment and lord, Spiritual Man, The SELF. Every mention of The Word, I AM, The SELF must therefore be taken to include the spiritual Triunity of the knowable God, Universe and Man.

Having traced the procession of I AM out of the unknowable Unity of God, we must comment on the relationship between them. For this is the subject-object relationship on the highest possible level and correspondingly subtle. The point to be noted is that I AM does not cease to be rooted in God's Unity when He comes forth into Triunity, any more than God abandons His Unity in expressing Himself in Triunity. The Word Whom God utters, The SELF Whom God sends forth into spiritual manifestation *is* Himself as He is spiritually knowable. Hence The Word, even when physically and not only spiritually embodied, expressly declares Himself to be one with God.[1]

This being so, it is plain that The SELF cannot fail to represent God perfectly. (In so far of course as Infinity can be represented). Hence the Bible speaks of Him as perfectly faithful and obedient to God.[2] He Himself incarnate declares the same quite explicitly and indicates why it is so. "The Son can do nothing of Himself, but what He seeth the Father doing".[3] He can do nothing of Himself, any more than an image can without its original. This being so, His very first act on being begotten must be to return, to project, to give Himself back to God. For it is only by such

[1] Jn. 10,30.
[2] Rev. 1,5; Rom. 5,19.
[3] Jn. 5,19; 5,30; 8,28 RV.

absolute obedience that He faithfully represents His infinite Original. It is indeed only thereby that He retains and maintains His very identity as The Word of God, The SELF, God become personal.

But The SELF would not be a true expression of God if He did no more than give Himself back to God. For this would not represent all that God accomplishes in begetting Him. He would not manifest the *creativity* of this supreme act of self-expression. He thus faithfully represents God's self-expression by in His turn projecting Himself to create His own image. Since He is Himself The Word, that is, the whole spiritual Reality, He must project Himself in corporeal manifestation. For there is, so to speak, no other aspect for Him to project Himself in but corporeal manifestation. So He creates the objective counterpart of His I AM. This is *I AM*, the ME vis-a-vis the I of His I AM; the one-many-corporate Triunity signified by the inverted triangle in the symbol; the Reality in its corporeal aspect.

We must now consider the projection of His I AM in corporeal manifestation, His self-expression in corporeal terms, and see what it especially means. Since His SELF faithfully represents God, He must project Himself to create His corporeal counterpart on precisely the same pattern as He Himself is begotten by God's self-projection. Let us recall this pattern. The Word comes forth from God's hidden Unity as I AM, and thereby gives rise to the Spiritual Universe of Knowing, Living Being, the fulfilment of which is its lord, Spiritual Man, The SELF. Therefore The SELF must also project His counterpart as *I AM*, from which arises the corporeal aspect of Knowing, Living Being, the Corporeal Universe, the fulfilment of which is its lord, Corporeal Man, The SELF. So the spiritual Word, I AM, comes to be represented by His corporeal counterpart, The Christ, *I AM*. But this tells us little, and so we must consider *what* He essentially does in thus creating His corporeal counterpart. This will become clearer when we see in the next section *how* and *why* He does it.

Let us begin by recalling that The SELF is the whole spiritual Reality, all that is spiritually knowable. We next recall that this consists of I AM "embodied" in the Spiritual Universe of Knowing, Living Being as fulfilled in Spiritual Man, The SELF. Putting these two together, we may say that The SELF represents all that is spiritually *knowable* in the act of spiritually *knowing* all. This "all" is of course His *SELF* in its objective aspect inclusive of all that corporeally *is*. This is the ME of His I AM, as we have put it. This is The Christ Who is The Word as corporeally knowable, rather as the earthward side of the sun is alone visible from the earth. It is worth stressing that the ME is as inseparable from I AM as I AM is from God. (And as the visible part of the sun is from the whole sun). The ME *is* I AM as far as we can know Him.

We have seen that He constitutes all that corporeally *is* in three main aspects. We have just introduced the first of these, His SELF as the prototypal corporeal Triunity. This is the innermost core of His Triunity where He is one with His subjective original, before having fully unfolded into the outermost corporeal conditions of space, time and change. There is none beside Him.[1]. The Holy Spirit, filling His I AM, represents in Him God. The realm of His activity, giving rise to the Corporeal Universe, represents in Him the Spiritual Universe. And the fulfilled work, of which He is lord and master, represents in Him Spiritual Man. So His corporeal Triunity is the exact counterpart of the spiritual one, as the inverted triangle is of the upright one.

We next see Him in His second aspect, the endless multitude and diversity of triunities. This aspect is due to the outermost corporeal conditions of space, time and change. As He extends downwards into these limitations, they necessitate the differentation of His prototypal Triunity into multitude and diversity.[2] A crude illustration might be the separation of light into the colours of the spectrum. Each of this multitude and diversity of triunities is an *I am*. The activity of each *I am* gives rise to that particle of the Corporeal Universe which is his body extending into his environment. And each fulfilled activity or work is a perfect Self. Their type is Jesus. Since space, time and change are boundless, the corporeal triunities are endless in their multitude and diversity.

Last of all we see Him in His third aspect as the multitude united in a corporate whole. Here He has gathered the endless multitude and diversity in one, without destroying the idividuality of any.[3]

---

[1] Isa. 45,21.
[2] Mat. 25,40; 1 Cor. 12,5.
[3] Eph. 1,10.

For this endless multitude and diversity-in-unity is the only manner in which the "unsearchable riches" of His Triunity, which in its primal aspect is beyond time and space, can be manifested in these outermost corporeal conditions.[1] He therefore leaves them outwardly individual *in* space, time and change, but inwardly draws them into unity with His SELF *beyond* space, time and change. They thus form one corporate body with an endless multitude and diversity of members. This is the Body of Christ, as the Bible calls it, the Universal Church in all its variants throughout all worlds and all ages.[2] So His "embodiment", begun at the summit of corporeal manifestation before it condenses into space, time and change, is fulfilled in literal embodiment. Here He stands fully unfolded, incarnate in the outermost corporeal conditions.

He expresses His SELF in these conditions by dwelling and working in an endless multitude and diversity of uniquely individual perfect Selves who are inwardly one *with* Him, and *through* Him one with each other. So through them, working in perfect harmony with each other, He fashions the corporeal Reality according to the pattern of the spiritual, and builds His City on earth.[3] Because He dwells and walks in it, in the words of the Bible, it is His Holy Temple.[4]

We have seen that the primary act of I AM is to give His SELF back to God. For it is only thereby that He maintains His identity as the Image, Word, SELF of God. In gathering together His own multiple corporeal image by inner union with His SELF, He therefore also unites the endless multitude and diversity of Selves with God. So through them the Glory of the infinite Reality is manifested in the outermost corporeal conditions of space, time and change, down to the very bricks and mortar composing the Holy City, and heaven and earth are filled with the Glory of God. So it everlastingly is to The SELF alone, and to those Selves who are one with Him.

[2]

Having outlined *what* The Word does in manifesting the Glory

[1] Eph. 3,8.
[2] Eph. 1,22 & 23.
[3] Isa. 45,12 & 13.
[4] 2 Cor. 6,16; Eph. 2,21; Rev. 21,22 & 23.

of God in spiritual terms, and as The Christ in corporeal terms, we must now consider *how* He does it. This will take us over the same ground again, but in more dynamic and detailed terms than before.

We begin at the point at which The Word is first begotten of God, the point at which He comes forth from the unknowable Unity of God and which we illustrated by the sunrise. As the first flash of light leaps forth with the appearance of the sun above the horizon, so The Word may be understood to emerge into spiritual manifestation from the cloud of unknowing and become spiritually knowable as I AM. So Being arises, in which I AM may be said to become "embodied". Let us call this point the First Moment of God's self-expression.

This First Moment of God's self-expression as I AM immediately reveals the first *facet* of His Personality. God has made Himself knowable essentially, by breaking His Unity for the sake of His Word's Triunity. He has thus broken and given Himself away in manifesting Himself as His Word. All other sacrificial acts must derive from this supreme act. We are familiar with them in the corporeal realm in many forms; they are found on every human level, from self-giving for the sake of an ideal to the body's self-giving in the physical act of reproduction. Hence we are prone to regard all self-sacrifice in terms of response to some desirable object, of desire to possess some spiritually or corporeally attractive thing. The Divine act of sacrificial self-breaking and giving away cannot be that. For it is made before there is anything for I AM to give Himself to. Its whole purpose is to give being to all things. It is therefore the purest act of will. Since it is prior to all things, it is perfectly disinterested; for the same reason it cannot possibly be thwarted. The first facet of The SELF to be manifested is therefore His inflexible Will.

The *quality* of His Will stands revealed at the same time. We have seen its purely sacrificial quality. We may now give it its proper biblical name of Love in its fullest sense.[1] This is not to be understood in terms of response to attraction, or desire to possess. Being prior to all things, His Love is thus best seen as the unconditioned and unconditional Will to sacrificial self-breaking and giving away, without reserve whatsoever. Since this is the prime reason

[1] Jn. 3,16; 15,13; 1 Jn. 4,10.

49

why the unknowable God manifests Himself at all, to pour Himself
forth for the sake of expressing His Infinity, S. John's description
of God as Love is illuminating.[1]

At the same time the *value* of His Will is also manifested.
His Loving Will is to break and give Himself away so that all
things may *be*. This is the most useful, the most usable act that
is conceivable. This is the most disinterested service that is conceivable. The usefulness of the act is the measure of its goodness.
So I AM manifests the perfect Goodness of His Will.

Having seen the First Moment of God's self-revealing procession
in spiritual manifestation, it is plain that this is also the corresponding Moment of His creative process. For, as we have seen,
all Being is then manifested, and proceeds from Him. As He
breaks and gives away His Being in the Loving Goodness of His
Will, He thereby ensures the essential goodness of all that is to *be*.
He founds the essential goodness of the knowable Reality in process
of being manifested.[2]

We now consider the Second Moment of God's self-revealing
procession, which is also the Second Moment of His creative process.
The Second is the immediate outcome of the First. The Will of
I AM is inflexible and must take effect. Its loving goodness makes
it irresistible. The Second Moment is thus the one in which His
Will is given effect, accepted without reserve. So the second *facet*
of I AM is manifested. This is His Heart which instantly accepts
and gives effect to His Will.

If His Will is to break and give Himself away so that all things
shall *be*, this creative intention can only take effect by His conceiving the idea of all things that are to *be*. We loosely speak of
ideas as conceived in the mind. But strictly, as any creative worker
more or less explicitly realises, ideas are conceived in the unconscious
depth of the self, which is not the mind. The mind only becomes
conscious of them in the process of trying to express them. That
unconscious depth of the self is what we may call the heart. And
it plays its part in the self solely because this is the objective
counterpart of The SELF. Next to His Will, therefore, I AM
manifests His Heart. In the boundless depth of His Heart He
conceives the all-inclusive, all-prolific, all-perfect Idea of all that

[1] 1 Jn. 4,8.
[2] Gen. 1,31.

50

is to be, of the entire knowable Reality. We may illustrate this by the sun's light touching off germination in soil or water.

In manifesting His Heart, I AM also reveals its *quality*. This issues directly from the quality of His Will. Since His Will is perfectly self-sacrificing, that is, perfectly loving, the Idea must be conceived in His Heart with infallible Wisdom. The Bible usually links wisdom with the heart. The Bible also gives wisdom the alternative name of understanding. This alternative is highly illuminating when referred to the Idea that understands or sub-stands the entire knowable Reality. No less illuminating is the fact that I AM declares Himself to be Understanding.[1] We may thus regard His wise and understanding Heart as the all-comprehending Idea of all that is knowable.

We customarily refer to God, and therefore to The Word and The Christ, as He. And though this is true in the same sense in which man is spoken of as he, we do well to remember that He is no less She. The Heart of I AM is His feminine, maternal aspect, as His Will is the masculine, paternal. If we call the latter His Creative Intention, we may call His maternal aspect His Creative Source, the spiritual womb in which the Idea of the knowable Reality is conceived. And since we are dealing with spiritual things, that womb is the Idea. Hence the Bible and other Scriptures usually refer to Divine Wisdom and Understanding as She. In this sense She may be called the Mother of God (knowable) and of Man (Spiritual and Corporeal).

The *value* of His Heart is revealed with its quality. This value too is the outcome of the value of His Will, which is Goodness. From what we have said of the feminine aspect of I AM, His Heart, it is clearly the *receiving* principle in relation with the *originating* one, His Will. Now true receptivity is not merely passive, but includes the vital capacity to attract. This capacity is essentially that of Beauty. Since this dwells in the hidden depth of the Heart, Beauty may also be called the Hidden, the Unknown, Mystery.[2] Though these three terms are seldom connected, we shall find it illuminating to use them interchangeably sometimes. With this relationship between the Will and Heart of I AM in mind, we may therefore say that the beauty of His Heart attracts His Will to give being to all things, and accepts His Will by conceiving

[1] Prov. 8,14.
[2] 1 Cor. 2,7.

the Idea of all that is to *be*. So His Heart stands revealed as supremely wise and beautiful, as in the previous Moment His Will stood revealed as supremely loving and good. Here His Being is manifested as Alive or Living, and all that is to *be* receives life. The knowable Reality in process of manifestation stands forth in all the Beauty of its Goodness.

Finally we come to the culminating Third Moment of God's self-revealing procession, which is also His creative process. The Third Moment is the outcome of the two previous ones, and is their fruit and synthesis. Here the Will of I AM, having been accepted and given effect to in His Heart, is fulfilled by being perfectly expressed. Having in the Loving Goodness of His Will broken and given away His Being, and having consequently in the Mysterious Wisdom of His Heart conceived the Idea of all that is to be, I AM now intellectually expresses that Idea. So the third *facet* of His SELF is manifested. This is His Knowing, His Mind. He stands forth as all that *is* or can *be*, the whole knowable Reality, in the act of knowing all. We may illustrate this with the sun which, having risen, in its full power brings growing things to their fruition.

In manifesting His Mind, He also reveals its *quality*. It follows from the quality of His Heart. Since the Wisdom in which He conceives the Idea of the knowable Reality is infallible, being the outcome of perfect Love, it is irrefutable. Thus the Mind that expresses it is all-powerful. This Power is absolute. All that is knowable *is* only because He knows it. Since He knows it in its perfection, it is perfect and would not oppose Him. Hence He declares Himself to be The Almighty.[1] *All* Power in the spiritual and corporeal realms is His alone. [2]

So also the *value* of His Knowing or Mind stands revealed. Since He *is* all that is knowable, as Knower of all, His Knowing must be absolutely true. For truth is the complete correspondence between that which *is* and the knowledge of it. He *is* The Truth. For He is all that *is* in the act of knowing all. Hence the Bible records Him incarnate as saying: "I AM the Truth".[3] Here His Living

---

[1] Rev. 1,8.
[2] Mat. 28,18.
[3] Jn. 14,6.

Being is manifested as Knowing, and all that is alive receives intelligence. The knowable Reality in process of manifestation stands forth in all the Truth of its Beauty and Goodness.

We may therefore say that in the Third Moment the spiritual embodiment of I AM, which began when He gave rise to Being, and continued when Being became Living, is completed in Knowing, Living Being. The works involved in this are represented by the Spiritual Universe. And the fulfilment of these works, which we have seen to be perfect in their Truth, Beauty and Goodness, is the Lord from Heaven, Spiritual Man. We may thus call Him the spiritual embodiment of Truth, Beauty and Goodness. He *constitutes* the entire knowable Reality in its spiritual aspect, and is its fulfilment in all its inexhaustible Truth, Beauty and Goodness. And in constituting all that is knowable, He *knows* all that is knowable in its unsearchable Truth, Beauty and Goodness. The all-inclusive object of His knowledge is thus the objective counterpart of His SELF, the ME of His I AM, The Christ Who *constitutes* the entire knowable Reality in its corporeal aspect.

So is fulfilled God's self-revealing procession into spiritual manifestation, which is also the process of His creation through His Word of its objective counterpart, all corporeal manifestation. So, in the language of the Nicene Creed, the Father begets the Son by Whom all things are made. So all things are essentially perfect because God knows them in that state, that is to say, has them in the Mind of His SELF in that state.

We saw in the previous section that, being the spiritual image or expression of God, I AM can do nothing of Himself. Having come forth from God, therefore, His first act must be to give Himself and all that He *is and has* back to God. The mode of His return into God must be governed by the fact that He is the image or expression of God. Therefore, His return must imitate His procession from God, but in the reverse order. Since we are ourselves images or expressions of I AM, the return into Whom is the great problem of our existence, His return into God concerns us not only theoretically but practically. We shall deal with the practical detail of the matter later. Here we need only state the principles involved. Since the Power of I AM derives from His Wisdom which derives from His Love, Love must be His prime motive. So from His Loving Will to give Himself **sacrificially** back to God flow the Wisdom of His Heart and the Power of

His Mind, wherewith to accomplish this. His Mind then guides His Heart and Will in carrying the sacrifice to its completion. He thus gives up His Mind, Heart and Will to God in three Moments in the reverse order of their procession. So He surrenders His Knowledge, then His Life, then His Being, and thereby is one with God beyond all. By giving up all to God, He receives all from God, and is thus able eternally to sustain His identity as the perfect Image, Expression, Word of God.

[3]

In showing *how* The Word manifests God in spiritual terms, we ended by mentioning His objective counterpart, The Christ, at the summit of corporeal manifestation. In the present section we shall try to show how The Christ, *I AM*, fulfils this manifestation. We shall see Him as He projects His *SELF* in the outermost conditions of space, time and change, whereby He comes to *constitute* the Reality in its *corporeal* aspect, as we have just seen Him constitute the Reality in its spiritual aspect. In seeing how He does this, we shall also see *why* He does it. Let us begin at the beginning.

Since He can do nothing but faithfully reveal God, He must project Himself precisely as God does in spiritual manifestation in the course of begetting Him. God makes Himself spiritually knowable in the act of breaking and giving away His hidden Unity and thus emerging as Triunity. Therefore, there must be a notional point at which the Unity of God stands poised and revealed at the summit of spiritual manifestation in the act of being broken into Triunity. Then follow the three Moments of His procession into Triunity in the course of which the Will, Heart and Mind of I AM emerge, become "embodied" in Being that is Living and Knowing, and finally stand fulfilled in Spiritual Man, The Word.

Therefore, there must also be such a notional point at which The Triunity, The Word, similarly stands poised and revealed at the summit of corporeal manifestation, before being broken into a limitless multitude and diversity of triunities, as demanded by the conditions of space, time and change. This is the point at which the objective counterpart of The Word first appears in manifestation. This is of course The Christ in the first of His three aspects as the single prototypal Triunity. Here The Word, in the act of knowing *all,* first knows Himself as *all.* Here the ME of His I AM first stands forth. Let us see Him at this point at which He exactly reflects His subjective Original, the I of His I AM. As I AM is "embodied" in spiritually Knowing, Living Being and fulfilled in Spiritual Man (The SELF), so *I AM* is embodied in corporeally Knowing, Living Being and fulfilled in Corporeal Man (*The SELF*). In this manner The Word's Triunity is first objectified as The Christ's Triunity of God's Holy Spirit, Corporeal Universe and Corporeal Man.

At this point The Christ stands forth corporeally manifested and embodied, but because He still verges with His spiritual Original, He is not yet incarnate in the outermost conditions of space, time and change. His descent into the multiplicity and diversity of the outermost corporeal conditions not yet having begun, He is still the unbroken counterpart of His spiritual Original. The visions of the prophet Daniel, S. John the Divine and many mystics may possibly refer to Him in this aspect. (Which He regains on re-ascending from the outermost conditions of space, time and change). This is His aspect, as we have seen, which is sometimes called the Cosmic.[1] Let us now trace His descent into the fulness of corporeal manifestation, where He becomes fully incarnate, so that He might fill all things.[2] We must remember of course that in doing so, He does not lose His prototypal triunitve aspect. (Any more than God loses His Unity in manifesting Himself as Triune).

Since He can but imitate God, His descent is essentially a continuation of the sacrificial self-expression whereby He Himself comes forth from God. Therefore the pattern of the sacrifice must remain the same. By the Loving Goodness of His Will, the Wisdom of His Heart and the Power of His Mind, He extends His objective knowledge of His SELF into increasing detail. His knowledge is, as always, creative. "Things are because He knows them". Each detail of His knowledge must therefore essentially be a triune microcosm of His own macrocosmic Triunity. "He giveth not the Spirit by measure".[3]

As His self-knowledge increases in detail, each resulting microcosm necessarily becomes correspondingly circumscribed, particular-

[1] Dan. 7,13; 10,5; Rev. 1,13.
[2] Eph. 4,9 & 10.
[3] Jn. 3,34 RV.

ised, separate from every other. The projection of His SELF ever further in corporeal manifestation essentially calls for His breaking and giving away into increasing multitudes and varieties of distinct Selves. These arrange themselves in a descending hierarchy and, as long as their embodiment is above the gross physical level of space and time, are called Spirits and Angels.[1] Finally His knowledge of His SELF, His self-knowledge, unfolds to the extremity of objectivity, causing the outermost conditions of space, time and change to appear. At this extreme point of His sacrificial self-expression, when the breaking of His SELF reaches a climax of creative agony, these Selves are no longer called Spirits and Angels but Corporeal Mankind.[2]

The ceaseless suffering of the sacrifice which The SELF undergoes in creating and upholding all things in their perfection form so large a part of the Christian scheme of the Reality, that we need only mention three familiar aspects under which it may be recognised. The first is S. John's vision of the Lamb slain from the foundation of the world.[3] The next is the death of Jesus on the cross, which is fairly commonly recognised as not only a sacrificial act in space and time, but as a manifestation of the everlasting archetypal sacrifice beyond. The one most familiar to Christians is no doubt the sacrifice shown forth in the Holy Eucharist, which signifies the self-giving not only of The Christ to the communicant but of the communicant in response to the Christ.

As the fulness and clarity of the symbolism in the Eucharist may not always be appreciated, it is worth drawing attention to. The archetypal sacrifice of The Christ is most clearly shown forth in the consecration and administration of the Bread, especially where round wafers are used. The great circle of the priest's wafer is broken. A circle is a universal symbol of wholeness, and the act of breaking the priest's wafer may be taken to signify The Christ breaking His all-inclusive SELF. But what the priest gives away to each communicant is, not one of the *fragment*s of the great circle, but the lesser circle of the people's wafer in its wholeness. This may be taken to signify the lesser Selves proceeding from His SELF as perfect microcosms of His macrocosm. As the

[1] Heb. 1,7.
[2] Ps. 8,5; Heb. 2,7.
[3] Rev. 13,8.

communicant receives the Sacrament, he receives power to give himself back to The Christ.

At the extremity of The SELF's differentiation into an endless multitude and diversity of Selves they are inevitably least like Him. So much so that they lose their awareness of Him as The SELF of all Selves, and therefore their True Self. They are thus as unlike Him as is possible without losing their essential identity as differentiations of His SELF. "The Light that lighteth every man that cometh into the world" shines in the darkness of their ignorance, uncomprehended.[1] Instead of ruling the corporeal realm, of which they are essentially the fulfilment and lord, they are unable to rule even their own body. Their selfhood, subject to the outermost corporeal conditions of space, time and change, is all but extinguished. The corporeal realm of which they are essentially master is their prison, a tomb in which in their ignorance they lie buried alive, so that they are as little *truly* human as is possible without being sub-human.

However, the darkness of their ignorance cannot destroy their essential identity as differentiations of The SELF. If only because darkness cannot destroy light. Every single one of them, in their endless multitude and diversity, is essential for the expression of His Truth, Beauty and Goodness in the outermost corporeal conditions of space, time and change. Each, even the least like Him, is indispensable for the manifestation of His unsearchable riches in the fulness of His incarnation. It is only in the very least of them indeed that He can be flesh in the depth of hell, as He is in the height of heaven in Jesus.[2] Hence He is not ashamed to call the least of them His brethren.[3]

At the nadir of their subjection to the corporeal realm they may be said to form the rawest material for His universal incarnation. He stirs within them to shape the raw material, thereby releasing them from their imprisonment in the outermost corporeal conditions and enabling them to rule these.[4] So He works through them without using them as tools, by awakening them to the presence of His SELF within them as their own True Self.[5] They can of

---

[1] Jn. 1,5 & 9; Third Collect for Evensong.
[2] Ps. 139,8; 1 Pet. 3.19; Eph. 4,10; Heb. 1,3; 8,1.
[3] Mat. 25,40; Heb. 2,11.
[4] Jn. 8,32.
[5] 2 Esdras 1,27; Jn. 1,9.

course do nothing without Him, as a sleeper cannot awaken without the stirring of his fully conscious self. Essentially He stirs them into wakefulness by attracting, drawing them to His SELF in their selves' depths by revealing some aspect of His Truth, Beauty and Goodness.[1] And the aspect He chooses is the one which best enables each Self to fulfil his destiny of showing forth one of the unsearchable riches of His Truth, Beauty and Goodness.[2] So He guards the spontaneity and sovereign freedom inherent in each as a differentiation of His SELF.[3] So in precluding the limitation of their endless diversity, He safeguards their spontaneous unfoldment of His unsearchable riches, and indeed preserves their very identity as differentiated aspects of His sovereign SELF.

His Power to draw them into union with His SELF without violating their sovereign freedom is absolute. For it springs from the infallible Wisdom in which He understands them.[4] This in turn springs from the Loving Will with which He gives Himself *for* and *to* them in pure self-sacrifice.[5] He irresistibly *charms* them into response to His Truth, Beauty and Goodness.

As they are touched by the Power of His Loving Wisdom and turn inwards towards His SELF in the depth of their self, so they awaken to their True Self.[6] In the words of the parable of the Prodigal Son, they come to themselves.[7] For their True Self is The SELF. In finding The SELF as their own True Self, they become one with Him. In so doing they also become one with each other, yet without losing their individuality. So each attains perfect corporeal manhood, which is corporate, and the measure of the stature of the fulness of The Christ.[8] Each dwells and works in the outermost corporeal conditions of space, time and change, but by interior union with His SELF and each other is as free from their limitations as He is beyond them. Their type is Jesus.

We may not go further into all that is implied by this, for this chapter is primarily concerned with the standpoint, not of the Selves,

---

[1] Jn. 12,32.
[2] Jn. 15,16.
[3] Rev. 3,20.
[4] Mat. 11,28.
[5] Jer. 31,3; Jn. 10,11; Lk. 22,19.
[6] Eph. 5,14.
[7] Lk. 15,11 et seq.
[8] Eph. 4,13.

but of The SELF. This is prior to theirs, which will be the concern of the next chapter. We must therefore see their awakening from His standpoint, as His gathering of them together in one Body in His SELF, so that He might fill all things.[1] What we essentially see in this is His *ascent,* which is the reverse of His *descent* into the outermost corporeal conditions of space, time and change. And the ascent is as hierarchical as the descent. We saw the descent as taking place through His Spirits and Angels. His ascent is through the sanctified corporeal Selves who are His Saints. His ascent through His Saints may be seen as the objective counterpart of His descent through His Spirits, in the course of which He fulfils His incarnation in the outermost corporeal conditions of all space, time and change.[2]

In the previous chapter we saw that God's return into His ineffable Unity is no mere vain reversal of His procession, but is the manner in which God manifests, expresses, unfolds His Infinity. In following His SELF's return into His prototypal Triunity after His differentiation into endless multitude and diversity, we see the unfoldment in more detail. In his prototypal aspect His incarnation is implicit, involved, folded up. In His fulfilled corporate aspect His incarnation is explicit, evolved, unfolded. As the former He alone knows Himself to be The All. As the latter The All knows it. So He is All in All.[3] It is as though every member of a perfect man's body were as perfectly aware of him as he is of himself. Hence the Saints are properly called Members of the Body of Christ, in which their communion with each other is so close that they are also members one of another.[4] This Body is the all-inclusive Society, the Universal Church in all its variants throughout all worlds and ages.

Because all are inwardly one with Him and with each other, He leaves each perfect freedom of self-expression. Yet however diverse this may be, because through Him each is in all and all in each, it must be perfectly harmonious and purposeful. So through them He unfolds His universal Truth, Beauty and Goodness in the endlessly particular terms demanded by space, time, and change. Through

[1] Jn. 11,52; Eph. 1,10; Eph. 4,10.
[2] Jn. 3,13.
[3] 1 Cor. 15,28.
[4] Eph. 1,22 & 23; Rom. 12,5; Eph. 4,25.

them He builds His Holy City throughout all worlds and ages.[1] Through them He dwells and walks therein.[2] So it becomes His Holy Temple whose very bricks and mortar unceasingly proclaim His Truth, Beauty and Goodness.[3] And so through them He causes the entire corporeal Reality to shine forth in Glory as the revelation of Infinity.

[1] Isa. **45, 12** & 13.
[2] 2 Cor. 6,16.
[3] Rev. 21,22.

Chapter 4

The MANY; The Selves

[1]

We now have to set out the threefold scheme of the Reality from the standpoint of The MANY, that is, the endless multitude and diversity of corporeal Selves, Corporeal Mankind. In them the self-expression of The ONE, God, begun in spiritual terms in The THREE, The SELF, is fulfilled in corporeal terms. In that sense their standpoint evolves from the two preceding ones in turn and includes them. So, in terms of our previous illustration of the sun, every point at which sunlight does its work in soil or water may be said to include the entire ray of the sun and ultimately the whole sun itself. Since the standpoint of the Selves includes the experience of *striving* to fulfil purposes and ideals, it may be called Ideal, just as that of The SELF was called Dynamic, and that of God Static or Changeless. Of course, the prior must always involve all that evolves from it; all that is manifested must be contained in that which is hidden.[1] God's changeless standpoint thus includes the dynamic and the ideal.

This being so, the standpoint of the Selves will be more clearly outlined if we do this in a stereoscopic manner, as it were. We shall describe it in terms of corporeal human experience in space, time and change. But we shall account for it in the light of the purpose of God and The SELF working through that experience beyond these outermost corporeal conditions.

If the corporeal Self is a triunity, we may expect his experience to fall into three main categories. The familiar terms Body, Soul and Spirit, which man is commonly said to comprise, give us the key to these categories. If we see the whole range of corporeal human experience as the process of awakening to True Selfhood

[1] Mat. 10,26.

in space, time and change, we may expect it to be spread over three main successive phases. Thus man's earliest experience, beginning at physical birth, is of his body and is characterised by consciousness. (Pre-natal experience is not distinct enough from his mother's for our purposes and is omitted). His next experience, beginning at psychological birth, is of his soul or psyche or selfhood and is characterised by self-consciousness. His third and culminating experience, beginning at spiritual birth, is of the Divine Spirit of The SELF and is characterised by the all-consciousness of I AM. In other words, corporeal man begins his existence in the realm of space, time and change unconscious of being a self at all, then awakens to selfhood, and finally to his True Self, which is The SELF in him. We shall speak of these three stages as childhood, adolescence and adult or full-grown manhood; but it must be understood that these terms indicate growth in selfhood and not merely in body.

Our outline of the corporeal human standpoint accordingly starts with man's physical birth, the point at which his individual experience as a merely conscious being begins. His birth ushers him into his first phase in the realm of space, time and change, and he experiences this as his childhood. What is the ultimate explanation of his birth which, as we have seen, is only to be found in the purpose of The SELF and of God beyond?

We know that in order to fulfil the expression of his Goodness, Beauty and Truth in corporeal terms, The SELF must become flesh in the outermost conditions of space, time and change. These conditions involve His increasing differentiation as He descends into them in the course of creating them by knowing them. Let us now examine this differentiation in a little more detail. Its essence is nowhere more clearly indicated than in the Parable of the Prodigal Son, and we shall follow this carefully throughout this chapter. According to the Parable, the younger son takes the initiative in leaving home. The father makes no demur, but divides his living and gives to his son the portion of goods that falls to him.[1] The father's concurrence clearly indicates complete unity and harmony of purpose between himself and his son. The Loving Goodness of The Christ's Will to break His SELF into manifold and diverse

[1] Lk. 15,12.

Selves for the sake of becoming fully incarnate is one with their will. Of course. For they are but differentiations of His own SELF, fragments hewn from the Rock that He is, in order that they may be reassembled into His Holy Temple in the outermost conditions of space, time and change.[1]

It follows that each freely chooses the particular manner in which he is to express corporeally the Truth, Beauty and Goodness of his spiritual Archetype. For the choice he makes is his own particular part in the overall purpose of The SELF. This means that the choice is made with infallible wisdom and is precisely the true one for him. Plato uses a myth to represent his view of how each Self chooses its destiny.[1]

Having chosen his particular destiny, his particular manner of showing forth the Truth, Beauty and Goodness of his Archtype, each then proceeds to work it out. According to the Parable, the Prodigal takes his portion of the goods that falls to him (and *in* him as we shall presently see) to a far country. This means as far from his home in The SELF as possible, into the outermost corporeal conditions of space, time and change. Each does this so that The SELF Who is above these conditions may, through him, become flesh in them. Therefore each becomes completely identified with these conditions. In order to do so, each has to forget his True Self. In Plato's language, he drinks of the Waters of Lethe. In the result he becomes so submerged by the limitations of these conditions, so much in bondage to their very elements, in S. Paul's language, that he counts himself as no more than a particle of them.

And so one such particle is prepared for him by his Creator, The SELF.[3] This particle is his physical body. It is the fine flower evolved from the elements of the physical universe and procreated by his earthly parents. It contains the essentials of the whole corporeal universe, down to its very elements. At the same time the body is prepared for him according to his choice of his

---

[1] Isa. 51,1; Jn. 2,21; 1 Cor. 6,19; Rev. 21,22.
[2] Timaeus. This principle holds good no matter what conditions in the corporeal realm are chosen; these are transformed as The SELF's overall purpose is worked out.
[3] Heb. 10,5.

destiny. Hence its particular constitution, as well as its home and general environment, is uniquely and perfectly suited for him as the vehicle in which he is to work out his destiny. His identification with his physical body begins at its conception in its mother's womb and is completed at birth.[1]

Such, then, is the fundamental explanation of man's physical birth. We now turn to the first phase of human experience that follows. Normally childhood experience must be predominantly pleasant. Its objective aspect may contain the pain due to helplessness. But its subjective aspect outweighs this, even if not mitigated by the protection of a normal home. The child lives immersed in its physical body, according to its senses and instincts, in irresponsible innocence. He has no self-conscious knowledge of good and evil, beauty and ugliness, truth and falsity. Hence he is untroubled by choice between these pairs of opposites, by conflict that follows choice, and by the deliberate sacrifice of one or other that ends conflict. He normally follows the lead of those upon whom he depends for his protection.

Individual human experience necessarily determines that of mankind as a whole. (Though the latter of course reacts upon it). For corporeal man as the differentiated aspect of The SELF is firstly individual and secondly collective. Individual childhood must therefore be reflected by an analogous collective period. This assumption is borne out by the presence in most of the great religious traditions of myths recording a Golden Age, a Paradisal state of innocence, a Garden of Eden. All these myths stress the satisfying security, carefree serenity and uncomplicated wholeness of man's existence following his first appearance on earth.

The explanation of this dominant feature of man's individual and collective childhood follows from what we know of the underlying cause of his physical birth. Having drunk of the Waters of Lethe and identified himself with his physical body, he is so wholly asleep to his True Self that he is not properly aware of being a self at all. He is not self-conscious in the full psychological and sociological sense. He can therefore enjoy the merely conscious life of the physical body in complete innocence without inner conflict. The Parable implies this happy state in describing the Prodigal

[1] Jer. 1,5.

as wasting his substance in the far country in riotous living without a qualm.[1] The most important explanation of this state is that it is necessary in order to allow the newly embodied Self to become fully identified with the physical universe which he is destined to rule and to transfigure. This state is also necessary as a period of rest, following the stunning blow of his separation from The SELF and fall into subjection to the physical universe, before He calls him to the supreme effort and suffering of working out his destiny.

The conventional Christian view of the Fall is as of a disaster. The Parable of the Prodigal Son does not justify such a view. On the contrary, as the son's reception on his return to his father shows, it treats his departure from home as a sacrifice for which he is richly rewarded. This supports our view that the Self's fall into subjection to the physical universe is no disaster but the sacrifice he undergoes in the course of fulfilling the purpose of his creation. In the words of the Te Deum, he abhors not the womb. His subjection is indeed his own peculiar part in the universal sacrifice which the whole manifestation of the Glory of the infinite Reality calls for, from God downwards. Hence the phrase, which is by no means confined to Christianity, "The Cross of Manifestation". The Cross in this universal sense, which begins for The Word as He comes forth from the infinite depth of God, begins for man as he comes forth from the spiritual depth of The Word. The following lines aptly express an enlightened man's understanding of his own fall.

"Into a dark leathern bag I was thrown,
And on a boundless sea I was set adrift,
Which was to me an omen of being tenderly nursed,
And the Lord God then set me at liberty".[2]

[2]

We now pass on to the second phase of human experience. It begins with psychological birth into adolescence and is characterised by self-consciousness. The fundamental reason of this development

---

[1] Lk. 15,13.
[2] The Welsh Bard Taliesin in the Mabinogion.

is that the True Self, sunk in the "deep and dreamless sleep" of the merely conscious life of the physical body, stirs to activity from the stupor of his fall.[1] This reason also accounts for the feature which dominates this second phase of human experience, in contrast with the first. The child has lived in the shadow of those upon whom it depends for protection, predominantly satisfied in its carefree security, serenity and irresponsibility. This pleasant state is now shattered by the adolescent's prime need for independence. As the adolescent, driven on by his growing self-consciousness, pushes out in quest for independence, his experience becomes increasingly composed of insecurity, conflict and the burden of responsibility. Thus, though he seeks satisfaction through independence, the more independence he wins, the less truly satisfied he tends to be. His experience is predominantly painful. His striving to be free at all costs is like a dream which has broken in on the hitherto dreamless sleep of his True Self. Since his True Self is not yet fully awake, however, his notion of liberty tends towards irresponsible license, and is thus a travesty of the True Self's sovereign freedom as Lord of the corporeal realm. His dream is thus better described as a nightmare.

Man's self-conscious phase obviously plays a far more crucial part in his pursuit of his ultimate purpose than the more passive phase of consciousness in childhood, and we should therefore consider it in a little more detail. As we have seen, the immediate effect of the awakening to self-consciousness is dissatisfaction with the dependent condition of childhood. However satisfying it was before, it now irks the adolescent as being intolerably limited, poverty-stricken and impotent. Which of course it is in relation to the sovereign freedom, unsearchable riches and power of the True Self. The Parable suggests this feature of adolescence in describing the Prodigal as having spent all and being "in want".[2]

The adolescent therefore begins his struggle to free himself from dependence and to "be himself", as he often significantly puts it. Since he is now conscious of being a self, he feels the need to give free play to its three main facets: mind, heart and will. His mind tends to be drawn to values which differ most from those

----

[1] Hymns A & M 642.
[2] Lk. 15,14.

that governed his childhood. Hence he is inclined to discard that which is traditionally proved to be Truth, Beauty and Goodness, and he falls into corresponding falsity, ugliness and evil. His heart is already a confused cauldron of newly-active feelings whose conflicting demands he cannot correlate and whose unfamiliar power he cannot control. What is unreal in his values increases this confusion. His will thus tends to be set on shifting short-term ends. In so far as these ends are based on unreal values, they yield him no real satisfaction. In so far as he pursues his shifting ends erratically, whatever satisfactions these yield him fail to reach fruition. And in so far as his ends are uncorrelated, and are thus liable to be mutually exclusive, they yield him actual frustration.

The adolescent is thus not only far less satisfied and happy than the child, but essentially far less free. For in depending upon the guidance of his more experienced seniors, the child not only tends to be in greater harmony with proved values but more free of the pressures of its physical body and environment. The adolescent is without this protection, and knows it. He is not only aware of these pressures, but is to some extent aware of being *subject* to them. This the child never is, not being conscious of being a self. In the result the adolescent tends consciously to identify his self with his physical body and the thoughts, feelings and activities associated therewith. So he *falls* into subjection to the outermost corporeal conditions of space, time and change, and his True Self becomes increasingly immersed in the corporeal realm. Henceforth we shall call this his *fallen* self, but always remember that it is essentially his True Self in its dreaming state and thereby subject to the corporeal realm of which it is essentially lord.

In the degree that the adolescent pursues unreal values, he inevitably blunders into difficulties and thereby subjects himself still further to the corporeal realm. Sooner or later his dissatisfactions reach the point of actual suffering. For unlike the child, which not being self-conscious strictly knows only pain, the adolescent knows himself to be in pain and therefore suffers. In the words of the Parable, he is not only "in want" but is aware of a "mighty famine".[1]

Since he is unlikely to seek relief from his difficulties at home, he "joins himself" to his fellow adolescents, if only because their

[1] Lk. 15,14.

problems are similar to his own.[1] But they, being newly self-conscious too, have their own difficulties. They are therefore equally "in want" and can offer him little help. The more self-conscious they are, indeed, the more likely they are to exploit his destitution for their own ends. According to the Parable, they put him to feed swine without reward, and prevent him from sharing even the husks the swine feed on.[1]

We have so far considered adolescent man as an individual. As in the case of childhood, he of course enters an analogous phase collectively. The point just reached in the Parable introduces us to society in its adolescent phase, and at the same time illustrates the basic reason why such a society, by increasing the difficulties of its members, subjects them still more to the corporeal realm. However obvious the effect of such a society may be upon its members, it is so important that it is worth pointing out. Where each member is bent on independence and on freely choosing his own values, mutual frustration is inevitable. Hence all must suffer and cause suffering to each other whether their chosen values are real or unreal. Such a society, lacking in cohesion, with competition constantly erupting into conflict, condemns its members to dependence upon the physical body and its passions, and these are inevitably reflected in the environment thereby created.

It is unnecessary to go much more into the endless tale of the suffering which self-conscious man inflicts upon himself and his fellows. The suffering obviously increases in proportion to the *intensity* of self-consciousness in individuals, social groups, and societies. And this increase is multiplied in proportion to the *numbers* of self-conscious individuals, social groups and societies. It is only necessary to touch on the effect of extreme self-consciousness. Here man's inhumanity reaches its climax, not only to other men, but most of all to himself. This is the antithesis of True Manhood. However rare the extreme forms of self-consciousness may be, as in mania, no one fully self-conscious can avoid all taste of the suffering this phase of human experience involves. For this suffering is his share of the sacrifice which the purpose of True Manhood demands of him.

[1] Lk. 15,15.

As one would expect, the more intensely self-conscious man becomes, the more closely he relates all that he knows to himself, that is, to his fallen self. So he places his fallen self in the centre of whatever he accepts as the Reality. But the centre of the Reality belongs to The SELF, and beyond Him to God. So man puts his fallen self in place of The SELF. By putting the part in place of the whole, the image in place of the original, he isolates himself, until he becomes "the abomination of desolation standing where it ought not".[1] So he completes his subjection to the corporeal realm by reducing himself to impotence. As he comes to learn more of the Reality, the more insignificant his own fallen self in the centre of the whole scheme is made to appear. Sooner or later, therefore, he finds himself in an impossible situation. He finds himself the vanishing point of an ever-expanding scheme. The result is that both he and the scheme cease to have any satisfying meaning for him. The desolation of the abomination is complete.

In describing the phase of childhood, we touched on its well-developed collective aspect, nostalgically remembered as the Golden Age of the past. We have just touched on the collective aspect of the phase of adolescence. It must be obvious that the separative effect of self-consciousness reduces this collective aspect to a rudimentary level, which ultimately withers away altogether. Man in the prime of adolescence co-operates with his fellows, of course, but he does so for his own individual ends, in the interests of his own fallen self. His co-operation is thus subject to endless conditions, and has no lasting or firm basis. The truly corporate life is therefore as impossible for him as it is for dry grains of sand to hold together.

We end our outline of this phase of human experience by accounting for its most characteristic features in the light of their basic cause. As we have seen, psychological birth is due to the True Self first stirring in the deep and dreamless sleep of childhood. Once this is recognised, the characteristic features of adolescence, culminating in full self-consciousness, become plain. One might say that the True Self's dreaming becomes ever more violent, until it erupts in nightmares. Increasing self-consciousness may therefore be seen as the increasing distortion of the all-consciousness of The

---

[1] Mk. 13,14.

SELF, of which the True Self is a differentiated aspect. The extremity of this state of distortion is thus the nadir of man's fall, where the fallen self is a travesty of the True Self, as a sleepwalker is of a fully waking man. Yet the very travesty points to the underlying True Self, which means that the fallen self can never lose *all* awareness of real values. Hence satire, unthinkable in the Golden Age, is savage in the degree that society is self-conscious.

It is necessary to mention only the greatest attributes of The SELF for the corresponding travesties of the fallen self to stand out. Others can easily be deduced from these. I AM is alone in His sovereign freedom; the travesty is isolated in his arrogant license. I AM gives in loving; the other takes in desiring. I AM is wise; the other is cunning. I AM is almighty; the other is violent.

The more the attributes and qualities of The SELF are travestied, the more the values they give rise to are distorted. The more the fallen self distorts Truth, Beauty and Goodness into falsity, ugliness and evil, the more it suffers. So the travesty of each value gives rise to its appropriate hell, first for the particular fallen self concerned, then for all others. The more intensely self-conscious the creator of the hells is, the more blind he is to their connection with his fallen self. But since hell is relentlessly hellish, it cannot be endured indefinitely.[1] Sooner or later he is bound to see the connection. For the Love, Wisdom and Power which give rise to Goodness, Beauty and Truth are never without their witness in any world.[2]

[3]

This brings us to the third and culminating phase of human experience. It begins with spiritual birth into adult, whole, holy manhood, and is marked by all-consciousness. We have just seen why, from the standpoint of the fallen self, every man must sooner or later seek liberation from hell. We now see the underlying cause of this. The True Self, having stirred in its sleep with increasing restlessness, awakens from the nightmare of self-consciousness in order to fulfil the purpose of its creation. (As the more

[1] Mk. 9,44.
[2] The principle of the "faithful remnant".

painful a nightmare, the more imminent the awakening). Therefore this culminating phase of human experience is governed by the joy of victory over suffering. This is, as we shall presently see, the synthesis of the opposites, the happiness of childhood and the suffering of adolescence.

Universal salvation is so far from being generally accepted among Christians, inevitably so where the all-inclusive universality of The Christ is not grasped, that its fundamental reason can bear with a little emphasis. Since The Christ comprehends all that *is* or can *be* corporeally, and since all Selves are differentiations of His SELF, they are *essentially* as He is, even in their fallen state. However long in their fallen state they may deny their True Self, they can no more lose it than a dreamer can lose his waking self. The very travesty presented by fallen selfhood proves the underlying presence of True Selfhood within. And the longer and more intense the misery brought about by the travesty, the closer at hand is the moment of awakening, of coming "to himself" in the words of the Parable.[1]

The manner of each fallen self's awakening is quite individual. Burdened by his self-consciousness, he somehow catches a glimpse of The SELF, as a dreamer might of daylight in his nightmare.[2] No doubt this glimpse comes to him through some witness of The SELF's Love, Wisdom and Power. The terms in which he recognises The SELF are irrelevant. They represent the Reality of The SELF as far as his newly-born spiritual insight allows. He recognises The SELF with whichever facet of his fallen self has been made most sensitive by suffering. His mind may be convinced of the Truth of The SELF as the all-comprehending Reality. Or his heart may be charmed by His Wisdom. Or his will may be stirred by the Goodness of His Love.

Whatever facet of The SELF he first discovers leads him to the others. So real Truth, Beauty and Goodness begin to dawn on him. His fallen self and its unreal values begin to fade from the centre of his scheme of the Reality. He begins to recognise his fallen self for the travesty it is of his True Self. Having thus personally discovered Truth, Beauty and Goodness through the

[1] Lk. 15,17.
[2] Eph. 5,14.

71

suffering caused by their opposites, the spiritually born man realises the basic cause of his misery. This is the separation of his self, through the Fall, from The SELF. This is the essence of sin. The Parable vividly suggests this awareness of deprivation. "I perish here with hunger", the Prodigal says.[1] And he abhors his fallen self which cuts him off from The SELF and thereby imprisons him in hell, and repents.[2] His existence begins to be dominated by the ideal of union with The SELF.[3]

So the immediate object of man's sacrificial departure into the "far country" is achieved, and he becomes fit to begin working out the purpose for which he is created. His suffering has shown him the Mind, Heart and Will of I AM, whereby He expresses Truth, Beauty and Goodness in spiritual terms. By paying this price man has made these values his own, as they never were when he professed them as a child. He now *possesses* them. So through The SELF, Whom he is beginning to know as his True Self, man becomes able to express them in corporeal terms. This is the purpose of his creation and his supreme destiny chosen before his Fall.

Then begins his struggle to attain his destiny, individually and corporately. If the "country" to which the Prodigal goes is "far", the journey home must be equally so. His will constantly flags, leaving his heart adrift, and his mind deluded. So he repeatedly seeks relief from the struggle by sinking back into bondage to his physical body and environment,[4] by escaping into violent sense experience;[5] by delusions of self-sufficiency.[6] And at each relaxation of the struggle he does not merely stand still but slides back.[7]

Each relaxation thus to some extent repeats his original Fall, and thereby subjects him to renewed suffering.[1] But since his True

---

[1] Lk. 15,17.
[2] Job. 42,6.
[3] Lk. 15,18 RV.
[4] Acts 7,39.
[5] Ex. 32,6.
[6] Deut. 8,17.
[7] Hos. 11,7.
[1] 1 Cor. 10,12.

Self has awoken, "the Waters of Lethe" are no longer there to dull the full pain of his fall. Each repeated fall is conscious and correspondingly painful. But this only makes the more certain his struggle to reawaken from the nightmare with renewed vigour. So each time man falls away from whatever degree of Truth, Beauty and Goodness he has attained, and suffers the corresponding hell of falsity, ugliness and evil, his suffering goads him to greater effort to "put off" his tormented fallen self. Each time it is further weakened. And so he not only recovers the ground lost by backsliding but discovers higher degrees of the supreme values. This is the pattern of his painful way to his father, in the imagery of the Parable, to take possession of the perfect Truth, Beauty and Goodness of his True Self, The SELF.[2] As suffering brings him to spiritual birth, so suffering fertilises his spiritual growth, and finally makes him perfect.[3] The father's embrace in the Parable signifies the attainment of union with The SELF.[4]

And yet the ultimate explanation of corporeal man's painful struggle is always the Love, Wisdom and Power of I AM drawing him to union with His SELF, and thus gathering together in one the endless differentiations of His SELF. This being so, and because their response is impossible without suffering, in drawing all men into His SELF, I AM suffers their pain in all worlds and all ages.[5]. So I AM has the power to give them all precisely the suffering they need for their individual and corporate spiritual growth and ultimate perfection. In thus ceaselessly drawing them to break ever further out of their fallen self into perfect freedom in His SELF, He enables them to fulfil their supreme destiny.[6] Hence any teacher worth his salt in some degree shares in the strain of his pupils' study, in the course of making them masters of the subject he is imparting to them. The Parable vividly illustrates this sacrificial sharing of The SELF in the working out of their destiny by all

---

[2] Lk. 15,18; Phil. 2,12 & 13.
[3] Heb. 2,10.
[4] Lk. 15,20.
[5] Isa. 63,9; Col. 1,24.
[6] Ezek. 37,12; Rom. 8,21.

selves. It describes the father as *running* to meet and embrace the son while he is yet *afar off*.[1] As far off as the far country, indeed, from which the son could otherwise never return. For the father's going forth to meet the son represents The SELF's descent through which the fallen self's ascent becomes possible.[2]

Essentially, therefore, suffering is the negative pole in all creativity, of which the positive pole is joy.[3] One is impossible without the other, in human experience, as any creative worker knows in the degree that his work is creative.

[4]

In outlining man's spiritual *birth* into truly adult, full manhood, we have necessarily seen him as an individual. But full manhood is attainable only corporately. Man's corporate, as opposed to merely collective, life is the objective aspect of his spiritual state. We must therefore end this chapter by touching on his spiritual growth, corporately, to full manhood.

We have seen man's struggle to attain this supreme purpose as his response to the Love, Wisdom and Power of I AM, whereby man attains ever higher degrees of Truth, Beauty and Goodness. We likened I AM to a teacher, which is indeed one of the commonest titles given to Him incarnate in Jesus. Through the great teachers of terrestrial mankind headed by Jesus, I AM teaches men to attain the purpose of their existence. Now all the teaching which enables man to "put off" his fallen self and to "put on" The SELF, in S. Paul's language, is summed up in one great law. This is to love God first and then his neighbour, to the uttermost.[4] S. Paul calls love the fulfilling of all law.[5] It could not be otherwise. For, as we have seen, all power to *do* anything creative derives from wisdom which derives from love. Therefore I AM clearly defines the love that is the key to all creativity. Love is sacrificial self-giving.[6] The key to man's most creative work, which is his spiritual

[1] Lk. 15,20 RV.
[2] Eph. 4,9 & 10.
[3] Heb. 12,2.
[4] Lk. 10,27.
[5] Rom. 13,10.
[6] Jn. 15,13; 13,34.

growth reflected by his corporate growth, is self-giving in love to The SELF and to all selves.

Since the spiritual life is necessarily corporate, the proper place to start our outline of spiritual growth is where it begins, that is, at spiritual birth. This is the point at which man first becomes aware, however dimly, of I AM as his True Self. Whatever his first impression of I AM may be, it must soon include a glimpse of His Love, and of His universal law of Love. Irresistibly drawn, he begins to respond.[1] His very first stumbling step to give himself to I AM begins to free his fallen self from the tomb of self-consciousness in which it is isolated. He begins to deliver his self from the prison of its fallen state in the course of giving himself, as his infant body was delivered from the womb at his physical birth. In the degree that he becomes aware of I AM as his True Self, he discovers Him to be the True Self of all other men too. He discovers himself and other men to be in I AM as differentiations of His SELF. To that extent, in embryo, he is one with I AM and through Him with all men.

So man's corporate life, the objective effect of his spiritual life, is born. The growth and consummation of his *corporate* life has fascinated him ever since he first became conscious of its possibilities. Every Utopia is a more or less detailed blue-print of its structure. But if it is the objective reflection of man's spiritual life, planning it alone can bring it no nearer. Fruit is impossible without root. So we shall not speculate on its detailed structure, fascinating though this might be. We believe spiritual training to be its indispensable prerequisite, and all we need do here is to outline its most essential aspects in the course of completing the subject of the present chapter, the Reality from the standpoint of the many Selves.

As the last section of chapter 2 suggests, this standpoint must have at least three essential aspects. We may again call the first qualitative. As an individual awakens to I AM as his and all other men's True Self, he is inevitably drawn into fellowship with others in a comparable state. As they come together and give themselves to each other in some form of supra-natural Love, each enables the others to break farther out of their fallen selves. So each self, hitherto exclusive of every other, now unites the others

---

[1] Hos. 11,4; Lk. 7,47.

with its own and is enriched thereby. Each individual retains his unique identity. But all the members of the fellowship are in some degree present in all others. So united, they think, feel and act as singly they cannot. To that extent they have broken out of mere self-consciousness and form a supra-individual body. To the same extent they have "put on" the all-consciousness of I AM and form a true part of His Body. It is the embryonic Body of Christ, and is to be found wherever individuals are united, not merely physically or psychologically, but spiritually; that is to say, through the Love, Wisdom and Power of I AM.

The process of unification continues from this embryonic stage on the same principle. As increasing numbers of fallen selves awaken to I AM in them and through His SELF become united with other selves, so the Body of Christ grows. In S. Paul's language, the Body increases according to the working of its parts in the love inspired by The Christ.[1] As the Body thus builds itself up in love, its corporate activity gains in power. Its members become correspondingly able to dominate, not only their own physical bodies, but their individual and collective environment. So the outermost physical conditions of space, time and change become increasingly adapted to the needs of all men's spiritual life. Not only are increasing numbers thus helped to spiritual birth, but those already born are enabled to come together with increasing numbers of their fellows. As individuals grow spiritually and the Body of which they are members thus builds itself up, so the two-sided process moves towards its consummation in the particular portion of space, time and change represented by one world, age and set of conditions.

Since Spirit transcends these terrestrial limitations, such progress in one portion subserves the increasing adaptation of all space, time and change to spiritual ends. The growth of the Body embraces other worlds, ages and conditions. It is consummated when the endless multitude and diversity of mankind, united in harmony, forms one all-inclusive Body embracing all worlds, all ages, all conditions. This all-inclusive whole, or holy social organism, is the corporate aspect of The SELF. And this Body, conterminous with the entire corporeal Reality, can alone *fully* express in corporeal terms the Truth, Beauty and Goodness of The SELF Who is the

[1] Eph. 4,7; 4,16.

76

knowable All. Yet each individual member of the Body, every single one of the endless multitude and diversity of fully adult men, is equally all-inclusive, because he is all-conscious. This is full manhood of which Jesus is the perfect type. So the knowable All is fully expressed by all that is knowable.[1] And so the Glory of God, the Infinite ONE beyond the knowable All, is manifested.

In outlining the quantitative aspect of man's spiritual growth and its consummation, we have inevitably touched on what may be called the qualitative one. We saw that as each man grows spiritually, so in union with others he gains mastery over his physical body and environment, and thereby adapts these to spiritual ends. His mastery is first of all reflected in the transformation of his physical body. This is raised from its original condition as a portion of the physical universe, the product of the evolutionary process, and becomes spiritualised.[2] It is thus renewed and recreated, as a building might be modernised, in accordance with the self's spiritual state, and thereby facilitates further spiritual growth. So the spiritually growing man, though still in the realm of space, time and change, ceases to be *bound* by these conditions, and arises from subjection to the decay and death inseparable from them. This progressive renewal and recreation of his body is the process of its resurrection and is fulfilled in its transfiguration. Then man shines forth as the sun.[3] So through his transfigured body he manifests in corporeal terms the Truth, Beauty and Goodness of I AM. And to that extent the corporeal Reality expresses the Glory of the infinite Reality.

The Christian should be the first to realise exactly why Jesus is the perfect type of glorified man, and thus the full incarnation of I AM, and of God beyond.[4] The measure of His perfection is His attainment of full spiritual manhood in a single lifetime. There appears to be no historical evidence of any other man having achieved in that span on this earth the crucifixion, resurrection and ascension into the glorified state. The Christian should thus be

---

[1] Col. 3,11; 1 Cor. 15,28.
[2] 1 Cor. 15,44 & 46.
[3] Mat. 13,43; 17,2; Rom. 12,2.
[4] Col. 2,9.

the first to see in His achievement a promise and guarantee of it being followed by all mankind.[1]

As individual men become glorified, this is reflected in the transfiguration of the Body which they compose. So the Body becomes able to renew and recreate its physical environment. As the scope of its mastery grows, it becomes able to spiritualise the physical world, transfiguring it from its original natural state into an increasingly perfect work of art. The crooked becomes straight and the rough ways smooth.[2] The desert becomes transfigured into the "Garden of the Lord".[3] Nature red in tooth and claw is tamed, until neither pain nor destruction have any place therein.[4]

As the Body of Christ grows in quality, it increasingly perfects the Garden of the Lord. The degree of civilisation which merits the name of Garden rises to that which merits the name of the City of God.[5] As the Body approaches its full spiritual stature in one world and age and condition, it overpasses the limitations of space, time and change. So it embraces other worlds, ages and conditions. Finally, when all its members are transfigured and glorified and are as Jesus, fully one with I AM and each other, the perfect Body of Christ extends throughout all worlds and ages and conditions. Then the Truth, Beauty and Goodness of I AM are manifested down to the very bricks and mortar of the City built by His perfect Body. This fulfilment of civilisation merits no less a name than the Temple of God. For God dwells and walks in it, incarnate in the all-inclusive company of His Saints in Glory.[6] Yet God is no less fully present to *each* than to *all*. So the entire corporeal Reality, now the Saints' perfect corporate work of art down to its smallest detail, expresses the Glory of the infinite Reality.[7]

These two aspects of the consummation of man's spiritual growth suggests one more that we must touch on. The quantitative and qualitative aspects led up to a point at which the outermost corporeal conditions of space, time and change are wholly governed

---

[1] Rom. 8,17.
[2] Isa. 45,2; Lk. 3,5.
[3] Isa. 51,3.
[4] Isa. 11,9.
[5] Rev. 3,12.
[6] 2 Cor. 6,16; Rev. 21,22 & 23.
[7] Isa. 45,13.

by glorified mankind united in I AM as His Body. At this point man, individually and corporately Holy as I AM is Holy, expresses through Him the Glory of God.[1] And God is all in all.[2] One may thus receive the impression that, man having conquered space, transcended time and spiritualised and transfigured all physical conditions, the corporeal Reality as such must vanish. Man appears to burn up the corporeal Reality in causing it to shine in Glory. I AM incarnate even declares that it shall pass away.[3] The very term *eschatology* confirms this impression.

But a little reflection must reveal that this cannot be the final end of the *entire* corporeal Reality as such. For if it were, God's self-expression would come to an end, and the Glory of His infinite Reality would cease to shine forth. And this is at least as contradictory as a cause without an effect, an author without his work, a sun without light. This paradox brings us to the last aspect we need touch on of the consummation of man's spiritual growth and therefore of his corporate aspect. This is the inexhaustible, endless fulness of its quantity and quality.

We begin by recalling that we have just set out no more than a single cycle of consummation. This is analogous to what in the Hindu Tradition might be called a Day of Brahm. We must now understand these cycles to be endless in quantity. But they do not endlessly repeat themselves. For this would limit their quality. They are as endlessly distinct in their quality as they are endlessly unlimited in their quantity. And "of the *increase* of" their quantity and quality "there shall be no end". For they represent the Infinite One's realm of self-expression, which the Bible calls His Government.[4] As we purge our understanding of limitations, God's expression of His Infinity and the infinity of His Expression take on meaning for us.

From our own present standpoint the Glory of God is plainly still very far from expressed on this earth. But we can imagine it fully expressed in some world, some age, some manner. So it is possible to appreciate that from the infinite standpoint of God there

[1] Lev. 19,2.
[2] 1 Cor. 15,28.
[3] Mk. 13,31.
[4] Isa. 9,7.

is no space, or time, or condition without the expression of His Glory. Therefore we can affirm with all those who are Holy as He is Holy, though not ourselves among them as yet, that Heaven and Earth are full of His Glory. And therefore we can express His Glory with our lips, though not in our lives as yet, and say that as it was in the beginning, it is now, and ever shall be.[1]

[1] Tersanctus and Doxology.

Chapter 5

The Process of The SELF's Incarnation

[1]

Having considered *what* man's spiritual growth is in essence, we must now see *how* it actually takes place. The present chapter thus forms the most practical stage of the first part of this book, and thereby links it with the next part which is wholly concerned with practice. The last chapter showed that man's spiritual growth is intelligible only in the light of the standpoint of I AM. For His self-unfoldment in corporeal manifestation is the underlying cause of that growth. And we have therefore seen it essentially as man's awakening to his True Selfhood in response to the Love, Wisdom and Power of I AM, whereby He becomes flesh in man, individually and corporately. How this takes place is of course also intelligible only in the light of the standpoint of I AM. Speaking generally, one may say that man grows spiritually as he assimilates the spiritual food I AM gives him, which is His SELF.

This being so, we will begin by summing up the standpoint of I AM set out in the previous chapters. We shall compress this summary as succinctly as possible, and at the same time put it into a form which is easily memorised, so that it becomes a formula, as it were, to be built into the mind. It will be found invaluable in helping us to assimilate the spiritual food which is I AM. For it is a synopsis of our whole exposition of the symbol on the fly-leaf and, since the purpose of our existence is to *be* in the flesh all that the symbol signifies, the "formula" is as important as the symbol. Both should become built into our mind, not only in the course of the exercises in Part II, but of our whole life.

As the "formula" is meant to represent the whole standpoint of I AM, it is based on His own words spoken in the first person.

The rest will be the briefest comments on these sayings in order to link them with the symbol. As we thus build His own words into our mind, we shall learn to have knowledge, not *about* His SELF, but *of* His SELF as our True Self.[1] Since the "formula" is the extremely compressed result of one person's meditation, as well as contemplation, it may not immediately become clear or easy to grasp. It may of course be varied, provided its essentials are preserved, to safeguard which the minimum of punctuation is given.

"I AM God . . . the Holy One in the midst of thee.[2] I AM the Lord, your Holy One.[3] I AM . . . the Beginning and the Ending . . . the Almighty.[4] I fill Heaven and Earth.[5]

Eternally in the Loving Goodness of His Will He breaks and gives away His SELF, thus founding the Goodness of His Infinite Reality being made known. So in the Mysterious Wisdom of His Heart He conceives the Idea of the knowable Reality fufilled in Man in all its Beauty and Goodness. So by the Power of His True Knowing, His All-conscious Mind, He *constitutes* the knowable Reality fufilled in Man in its spiritual aspect in all its Truth, Beauty and Goodness. And immediately, by this Knowing, He *creates* its objective counterpart, the knowable Reality fulfilled in Man in its corporeal aspect in all its Truth, Beauty and Goodness. So He is the Beginning, the Source of all things invisible and visible.

By His perfect Love, Wisdom and Power alone He upholds the knowable Reality fulfilled in Man in both its aspects in all its Truth, Beauty and Goodness. He does so by *constituting* the Reality fulfilled in Man in its spiritual aspect in all its Truth, Beauty and Goodness; and by knowing and thus *creating* the Reality fulfilled in Man in its corporeal aspect in all its Truth, Beauty and Goodness. So He is the Ground of all things invisible and visible.

By His perfect Love, Wisdom and Power alone He draws into His SELF the Reality fulfilled in Man in its corporeal aspect, through Corporeal Man. And in so doing, He constitutes the Reality fulfilled in Man in its *corporeal* aspect in all its Truth, Beauty and Goodness, by Corporeal Man. So He is the Ending, the Fulfilment of all

[1] 2 Esdras 1,27; Col. 1,10.
[2] Hos. 11,9.
[3] Isa. 43,15.
[4] Rev. 1,8.
[5] Jer. 23,24.

things invisible and visible. So He fills Heaven and Earth. So Heaven is His Throne and Earth is His Footstool.[1] He fills **Heaven** by His SELF with Truth, Beauty, and Goodness. He fills Earth by His People which He formed for His SELF that they might set forth His Praise with Truth, Beauty and Goodness.[2] And so Heaven and Earth are full of His Glory.[3]

Having given the "formula", let us dwell on it in order to absorb its meaning. Its lack of punctuation, which is meant to guard against ambiguity, may not make it easy to grasp immediately. Then let us make the first use of it in preparing to consider the assimilation of the spiritual food which is I AM. In defining Corporeal Man's place in the scheme of the Reality, the "formula" impresses upon us our complete dependence upon this spiritual food. Man can no more do anything truly positive without I AM, least of all represent Him in corporeal terms, than an image can stir in a mirror without its original. Just as He Himself can do nothing without His Supreme Original, God, The Infinite.[4] For as He spiritually manifests God, so man corporeally manifests Him. At the same time the "formula" points us to the incalculable amount mankind has to do through Him, that is to say *all things* in the corporeal realm, in S. Paul's language.[5] In preparing to assimilate the spiritual food, which is I AM, we are therefore called to be, not passive, but supremely and vitally receptive. Essentially, our highest activity must be to stop our fallen self from acting, and submit to be *acted through* by I AM.

We now have to consider how we assimilate spiritual food. In the first place that depends, of course, upon how I AM feeds us with His SELF. The sacraments present in some form in most religious systems point us to the answer. In our own system, in the Holy Eucharist The Christ feeds the communicant with the spiritual food of His Body and Blood. In instituting the Sacrament, Jesus used the symbolism familiar to the Jews, to whom the flesh of a creature signified its essential nature and its blood its life. The Body and Blood of The Christ thus signify His Essence and Life.

---

[1] Isa. 66,1.
[2] Isa. 43,20 & 21.
[3] Tersanctus.
[4] Jn. 5,19 & 30.
[5] Phil. 4,13.

And in receiving the Sacrament the communicant is spiritually fed with what we have called the Living Being of I AM.[1]

We know that the communicant receives this spiritual food by faith. But that does not tell us how I AM spiritually feeds him, and all others who receive sacramental food in different forms, including some without any visible sign at all. We shall seek the answer to this question in the most universal terms we can find, that is, in the scheme of the Reality which we have deduced from the symbol with the aid of the Chaldean Oracle. We shall find that the Bible attests the truth of our answer very clearly.

[2]

The opening words of the oracle give us the key to the answer we seek. "The ONE spake, and immediately The THREE came forth and became The MANY," it declares, "and The MANY returned again through The THREE into The ONE". We know The THREE to signify the Triune Reality in its spiritual aspect as The Word, The SELF. We may take it, therefore, that The Word is begotten by being *spoken*. And if The SELF is begotten by being spoken, He must be upheld and fulfilled in union with God by the same means. We know that The SELF can do nothing but imitate God. It follows therefore that The SELF in His turn creates, upholds and fulfils the Reality in its corporeal aspect, the endless multitude and diversity of corporeal Selves in their individual and corporate aspects, also by speaking them. Or more strictly, by speaking or uttering His Knowledge of them.

We now see how I AM feeds corporeal mankind with His SELF, thereby enabling them to grow spiritually and fulfil the purpose of their creation. Having created them by speaking them, that is by His Words, He spiritually feeds them by His Words, and enables them to grow to spiritual perfection by His Words.

Clearly therefore nothing can equal the practical importance for corporeal mankind of the Words of I AM as recorded in all the scriptures and for Christians particularly in the Bible. He Himself

[1] It is interesting to recall that, though Jesus used symbolism familiar to the Jews, it was similar to that used in the Egyptian and Greek systems, in which "communicants" were spiritually fed by the breaking and distribution of Osiris and Dionysius respectively.

leaves no doubt on that score. "Heaven and Earth shall pass away," He declares in Jesus, "but MY Words shall not pass away".[1] His Words transcend not only the corporeal realm, but the spiritual realm. Not only because He is Lord of both, but because these Words are ultimately not His but those of the unknowable God beyond all.[2] In that sense they are co-equal with His SELF, the living spiritual aspects of His very SELF. "The Words that I speak", He declares, "they are Spirit, and they are Life".[3] They are not symbols *of* Spirit and Life, let us note, but actually *are* Spirit and Life.

Being aspects of His very SELF Who is the Beginning and the Ending, these Words, and the Spirit they are, thus actually create, uphold and fulfil all things in the spiritual and corporeal realms. For it is He Himself Who works in these Words. Here too He leaves no doubt on that score. "I will . . . perform MY Good Word", He declares.[4] "I watch over MY Word to perform it".[5] "I will speak, and the Word that I shall speak shall come to pass".[6] Many other Sayings could be cited. He often indicates the particular work performed by His Words. Space allows us to mention only one instance of each great category of His work: creation, upholding and fulfilment. "The earth, and . . . the heavens: when I call unto them, they stand up together".[7] "As the rain cometh down, and . . . watereth the earth, and maketh it bring forth . . . so shall MY Word be that goeth forth out of MY Mouth".[8] "Ye are clean through the Word which I have spoken unto you".[9]

We may be questioned for giving such transcendent importance to the Words of I AM, especially in an age when written and spoken words are so plentiful and so carelessly used that they are largely ignored. If so, it should be noted that our view is borne out by the writers of several Epistles. Since these contributors to the Bible are accepted as inspired by the Holy Spirit, so that the

[1] Mk. 13,31.
[2] Jn. 14,24.
[3] Jn. 6,63.
[4] Jer. 29,10.
[5] Jer. 1,12 RV.
[6] Ezek. 12,25.
[7] Isa. 48,13.
[8] Isa. 55,10 & 11.
[9] Jn. 15,3.

85

Bible as a whole is (rather loosely) called the Word of God, He
Himself may be said to confirm the importance of His Words by
these witnesses. Space allows us to mention only a small selection.
The following suggests the dynamic quality of His Words in general.
"The Word of God", states the Epistle to the Hebrews, "is living,
and active".[1] The following indicate respectively the creating, upholding and fulfilling work performed by His Words. "The worlds
were framed by the Word of God", states the same Epistle.[2] It
also describes God as "upholding all things by the Word of His
Power".[3] No one expresses the action of the Words in fulfilling
the Divine Intention more clearly than S. Paul. "I commend you
to God, and to the Word of His Grace", he declares, "which is able
to build you up, and to give you an inheritance among all them that
are sanctified".[4]

Enough should now have been said to establish our view that it
is essentially by His Own Words that I AM spiritually feeds corporeal man with His SELF, until He becomes flesh in him, thus
fulfilling His purpose in creating him. It follows from this that
essentially man receives I AM by means of His Words which are
Spirit and are Life. For His Words *are* His Living Spirit. They
are His Holy Spirit. Man receives the inspiration of His Holy
Spirit by means of His Words.

Such a view, resting as it does on the literal acceptance of biblical language, may possibly seem over-simple. The mystery of the
gift and reception of God through The Christ is usually regarded
as penetrable only in some kind of sacramental terms. God's
communion with man is usually veiled in metaphor or analogy. We
will therefore explain our view, which seeks to penetrate beyond
metaphor or analogy, by showing that communion between all selves
follows a similar pattern. Necessarily so, since all communion must
derive from the archetype we have mentioned.

Let us take the example of the communion between, say, a doctor
and his patient whom he wishes to restore to health, a leader and his
followers whom he wishes to uphold in some difficult enterprise,
a teacher and his pupils whom he wishes to perfect in their subject.

[1] Heb. 4,12 RV.
[2] Heb. 11,3.
[3] Heb. 1,3.
[4] Acts. 20,32.

In each case the active party in some degree gives or projects his self into the relatively passive ones. He starts by willing to impart something of himself for the benefit of those who look to him for aid. This intention evokes in his heart the feeling in which he conceives the idea of what should serve them best. He then expresses the idea in his mind by some concept, some thought of the benefit to be given, and utters this in words, silent, spoken or written.

The giver's self-communication is of course received in an inverse order. It starts with the recipients' acceptance of the words which utter the giver's thought. So their minds receive the thought. The thought evokes the feeling of the underlying idea in their hearts. The feeling then stirs their will to the appropriate act. So their will carries out the giver's will. At that point his words may be said to live and act in them. And to that extent he himself "dwells and walks in them". To that extent he is incarnate in them. But he is present in them in *their* terms, not his.

If this is the basic pattern of human self-giving and receiving, it can only be so, as we have seen, because its archetype is the self-giving of I AM to corporeal mankind. Let us then study the archetype, taking note of the evidence for our view in the Bible. We have seen that in communion between human selves words more or less accurately represent thoughts, feelings and acts of will. We may take it therefore that each Word or Saying of I AM represents some Thought in His Mind. This Thought expresses the Feeling of some Idea conceived in His Heart. And this Idea is conceived as a result of some act of His Will. We know that His Will is perfectly Loving in its Goodness, His Heart irrefutably Wise in its Beauty, His Mind irresistibly Powerful in its Truth. His Sayings must therefore utter His Thoughts with perfect accuracy, and in fact *be* His Living Spirit in a communicable form.

Let us now trace man's reception of His Sayings, whereby I AM becomes flesh in him. His reception starts when man truly hears the Sayings. He must therefore *listen* to them, not as he does to words in general, but with the utmost attention. Hence I AM incarnate in Jesus teaches him to let His Sayings sink down into his ears.[1] In so far as he "learns, marks and inwardly digests them", he begins to receive them in his mind.[2] So the Divine Thoughts

[1] Lk. 9,44.
[2] Collect for Advent 2.

they utter, and to that extent the Mind of I AM, are given to him.[1] As he lets the Sayings *abide* in his mind, thereby holding in his mind the Divine Thoughts, these begin to evoke in him the Feelings of the Ideas they express.[2] So he begins to receive the Sayings in his heart. And the Divine Ideas, and to that extent the Heart of I AM, are given to him. Hence I AM explicitly teaches him to lay His Words up, as He says, in his heart and in his soul.[3] As he does so, the Divine Feelings begin to stir his will to action.

We must carefully consider this action of man's will. Outwardly *his* will is in action. And he acts in his own uniquely characteristic manner. But inwardly it is not his will that is in action. For its driving power are the Sayings which have set it in motion. Essentially it is the Will of I AM, uttered by the Sayings, that is in action. Thus the Sayings may fairly be said to live and work in man. We have already quoted I AM as declaring that He watches over His Word to perform it.[4] His other Sayings in this connection will assume additional significance in the light of our present study. Perhaps most vivid of all is S. Paul's assertion that the Word of God "worketh in them that believe".[5]

So I AM feeds man with the Spiritual Bread of His SELF. So by His Sayings living and acting in corporeal mankind, the single inexhaustible Will of I AM is done on earth in endlessly many and diverse ways.[6] And so the Kingdom of Heaven comes on earth. As the part played by the Divine Sayings in its coming is understood, so the Parable of the Sower gains in significance. The "Word of the Kingdom" mentioned in the Parable is commonly taken to mean the Bible in general, or more specifically the teaching of Jesus and the prophets. No doubt it does mean that. We understand it also in the more literal and exact sense to mean the actual Sayings which, by becoming flesh in man and working in him, accomplish the Will of I AM on earth. The practical value of the Parable for the spiritual life can hardly be exaggerated.[7]

[1] 1 Cor. 2,16; Phil. 2,5.
[2] Jn. 15,7.
[3] Deut. 11,18; Ezek. 3,10.
[4] Jer. 1,12 RV.
[5] 1 Thes. 2,13.
[6] Heb. 4,12 RV: Lord's Prayer.
[7] Mat. 13,3—23; Mk. 4,3—20; Lk. 8,4—15.

[3]

Having mentioned what appear to be the essential principles governing man's spiritual growth, or conversely The Word's incarnation by means of His Words, we must now look at the process as it actually takes place in this world. Since we are concerned with its pattern rather than historical detail, we need not try to date its beginning. It must begin sometime after the Golden Age of man's collective childhood has passed away, and we may for convenience place it where we first know something of man's spiritual life from the scriptures which underlie the great religious traditions. If we have grasped the principles correctly, the pattern must be substantially similar in other worlds and ages.

We shall appreciate the essence of man's spiritual growth best if we include in our outline of the pattern, not only how man tries to receive the Words of The Word, but how he tends to fail, and finally how his failure turns to his profit. This three-stranded dialectical pattern of spiritual growth is, as always, intelligible only in the light of the standpoint of I AM. For man's painful growth is his increasingly conscious response to the Love, Wisdom and Power of I AM, from Whose standpoint he is already fully grown.

We begin then with the first of the three strands. As we saw in the previous chapter, every man owes his spiritual birth to hearing, in the misery of his self-consciousness, some Word or Saying of I AM, and thereby catching a glimpse of His Living Reality. In the degree that he then seriously sets out to receive the life-giving Spirit of the Sayings in mind, heart and will, he *has* them.[1] To this extent being raised up, as though a watchman on a tower, he is able to transmit them to others.[2] He can of course transmit no more than he *has*. Thereby fitted to lead others spiritually, he attracts disciples. Inevitably, for in the degree that he *has* the Words, The Word is flesh in him and through him draws men into His SELF. In so far as the disciples receive the Words, they too are raised up as watchmen, with corresponding power to transmit the Words to their own disciples in turn. So by means of the

[1] Jn. 6,68.
[2] Ezek. 3,17.

89

Sayings the spiritual birth and growth of the watchmen, more usually called sages or prophets or teachers, progressively inspires the great religious traditions and spreads them into the general body of mankind. And so from the Sayings, from "the sincere milk" of the Word, flow all the scriptures, primarily addressed to the human mind; all the sacramental systems, primarily addressed to the human heart; all the commandments, primarily addressed to the human will.

So mankind grows spiritually and "in the fulness of time" reaches the point at which the greatest of them is able to receive and to transmit the Spirit of the Sayings in its fulness. These Words, which are Spirit and are Life, express the whole Mind, Heart and Will of I AM. He alone can utter them. He therefore becomes flesh in Jesus. Or conversely, Jesus is the first corporeal man in this world, so far as is known, to receive the Spirit of the Words so fully as to *have* them wholly, and therefore to *be* The Word Who utters them in the flesh.[1] This being so, His power to transmit the Spirit of the Words in its fulness to others is complete.

That which spiritually growing mankind has foreseen with increasing clarity, as is reflected in the myths and prophesies of the various religious traditions, is fulfilled as a historical fact in the first corporeal man known to attain his ultimate destiny in this world. Jesus demonstrated His complete awakening to The SELF as His True Self, and therefore to the presence of I AM incarnate in Him, by dying, arising and spiritualising His physical body in the sight of His disciples.[2] They actually behold Him manifest the Glory of God in this world.[3] He gathers His disciples into a body so that they may receive and transmit the full Spirit of His Words.[4] So they constitute the embryo of the Body of The Christ, the embryo of the All-inclusive or Holy, the Universal or Catholic Church which is destined to build the City of God in this world, and in all its endless variants ultimately the Temple of God in all worlds.

Since the Body's whole spiritual condition, inspiration and power to fulfil its mission ultimately depend upon its members' ability

---

[1] Jn. 6,68; Jn. 1,14.
[2] Lk. 24,51; Acts 1,9.
[3] Mk. 9,2; Jn. 1,14.
[4] Jn. 16,13.

to receive and transmit the Spirit of the Sayings, it has necessarily guarded and applied the principles which govern this vital process. One might call it the spiritual metabolism of corporeal mankind. If space allowed, it could be shown how any spiritually vital period of the Church, and the consequent progress of civilisation, directly depends upon these principles being best understood and applied. For instance, in Europe the mediaeval age of faith was followed by the age of progress called the Renaissance. We will now outline what we regard as the most fruitful application of these principles.

We begin with some essential points to be constantly borne in mind by anyone who aspires to receive the Spirit of the Words so fully as to *have* them, preparatory to trying to *do* anything. First, he must be prepared to put this work before any other, no matter how he earns his living. For this is the greatest work he can do for himself and for all mankind. Next, he must keep his mind, heart and will in the proper condition, fitness and purity for the reception of the Words. Therefore, he must be familiar with the Bible and the theology derived from it, so as to know as much as possible about the Words; must make full use of the most spiritual forms of devotion available to him, especially the Sacraments; must keep the Commandments as strictly as he can, and be as morally perfect as he can. Then he must never forget the order in which each Saying can alone be most effectively received, no matter how eager he is to progress. Since corporeal man's mind gives him his first conscious contact with I AM, the Spirit of His Sayings can only be fully received, first in the mind, then in the heart, then by the will, and in no other order. For this is the order in which The SELF becomes flesh in corporeal selves. Finally, he must never forget that, however much each Saying may differ in content from others, all are uttered by I AM and are but aspects of His Holy Spirit. The "formula" set out on page 82 is invaluable for this purpose.

We now come to the actual reception of each Saying. The aspirant concentrates and stills his mind in order to achieve the highest degree of receptivity. He stills his own thoughts, even the most exalted inspired by the Saying he seeks to receive, and tries to let nothing but the Saying in its purity dwell in his mind. For his own thoughts, however exalted, differ categorically from those of

I AM.[1] There is no better way of filling his mind with the Saying than to repeat it mentally just fast enough to keep other thoughts out. As he thus fills his mind with the actual Saying alone, he begins to receive it in his mind, and the divine Thought uttered thereby.

He next enters the more difficult stage of receiving the Saying in his heart. He prepares to experience, to *taste* the Divine Feeling of the Idea expressed by the Divine Thought he has just received.[2] He stills all his own feelings, however exalted, and tries to taste nothing but the Feeling that lives in the Saying, the Feeling with which the Saying is alive. To silence his own feelings is even more important than to silence his own thoughts. If he tried to induce any exalted feelings in himself, believing these to approach the Feeling enshrined in the Saying, they would be a much greater travesty of the Heart of I AM than his own thoughts would be of the Mind of I AM. For the fallen self's heart is farther from the Heart of I AM than its mind which, as we saw, is the first point of contact between spiritual and corporeal selfhood. The aspirant thus tries to surrender his whole capacity for experience to the Divine Feeling living in the Saying, allowing this ineffable Feeling to distil into his heart and to come to life in him in place of his own feelings.

Lastly he enters the third and most difficult stage in the reception of the Saying, its reception by his will. Here the Saying, having come to life in his heart, is to become active in him, to begin working in him.[3] So he begins to possess, to *have*, and to *be* the Saying, which thus becomes flesh in him. What actually begins to be flesh in him is of course no more than what has come to life in his heart after having informed his mind. He stills his own will, however well-intentioned, and tries to submit to the Divine Will expressed by the Saying. To silence his own will is most important of all. He must not use his own will to give effect to the Saying. To do so would be to act out the role of I AM, which would be the greatest travesty of all. For the fallen self's will is even further removed from the Will of I AM than the heart. The divergence between fallen and true selfhood is greatest of all in the case of the will. The aspirant must use his will solely to give "free course" to

[1] Isa. 55,8.
[2] Ps. 119,103; Heb. 6,5.
[3] Heb. 4, 12 RV; 1 Thes. 2,13.

the Saying, as I AM incarnate significantly puts it.[1] He must use his will to be used by the Saying. He must use his will to stop willing, so that the Will of I AM is done in him by His Saying working in him.[2]

[4]

We now come to the second strand of the pattern of man's spiritual growth. Having shown what we regard as the most fruitful way of receiving the Divine Sayings and the inspiration of their Spirit, we shall now consider the most common perennnial failures to do so. Failures in receiving the Sayings of course result in failures in transmitting them. For a man can only pass on what he has received.[3] All such failures are of course due to the self's fallen condition, and are in that sense inevitable.

The first failure is due to violation of the proper order in which alone the aspirant can receive the Sayings so as to *have* them and so to incarnate them. Thus, his reception of the Sayings may stop at the mind. Having grasped something of their significance, he is left fascinated, giving himself up to theological and philosophical speculations (which are perfectly in order elsewhere).[4] Hence he never seeks to taste the Feeling alive in the Sayings, and never receives them in his heart. The Divine Ideas uttered by them do not come to life in him. Unmoved by experience, his will inevitably remains inert. Or he may receive the Sayings in the heart but allow them to remain there. Having tasted the Feeling alive in them, he may become a quietist revelling in spiritual experience, leaving his will inactive. Or he may duly accept the Sayings with the will but, instead of thereby letting them act in him, use his own will to act them out, thereby distorting all that they represent.

Or again, he may be so intent on action that he violates the proper order of receiving the Sayings in the opposite direction. So he may try to act out the Sayings before having tasted the Feelings that live in them, and thus entirely fail to understand the Ideas they represent. His act will then be a still greater distortion than already

---

[1] Jn. 8,37 RV.
[2] 1 Thes. 2,13.
[3] 1 Cor. 4,7.
[4] 2 Tim. 3,7.

mentioned. Or he may try to taste the Feelings that live in them before his mind is sufficiently informed, and so his experience will be self-induced fancy.

The second failure is due to the aspirant's inability to still his own mind, heart and will when trying to receive the Sayings. Hence he thinks *about* the Sayings instead of concentrating *on* them, he intrudes his own feelings instead of tasting the Feeling they enshrine, he uses his own will to act them out instead of letting them act in him. The result of this intrusion of his own mind, heart and will into his attempt to receive the Sayings in their purity is to cut himself off from their true significance, content and power. In effect, he makes of them "idols according to his own understanding", in Hosea's language.[1]

The third and probably the commonest failure to receive the Sayings fully is due to a more insidious form of idolatry. As we have seen, every man attracts disciples in the degree that he *has* the Sayings. For, in plain language, he is in that degree inspired. Now the more inspired he is, the more his disciples are tempted to look to him to give them the Sayings rather than to I AM. So, instead of receiving the Sayings in their purity, and letting them speak for themselves and do their own incomparable Divine work, the disciples are tempted to receive them as expounded by their teachers. In so far as they give in to this temptation, they thus receive a second-hand dilution of the Sayings. And when they become teachers in their turn, they pass on these dilutions to others. So these dilutions spread in ever-widening circles, tending to ever-increasing distortions of the pure Spirit of the Sayings.

These three most common failures to receive and transmit the Sayings in their purity, perennially present throughout man's spiritual growth, account for most of the dilution and distortion of the Holy Spirit at work in corporeal man. These failures all originate from the inevitable tendency of every man, short of perfection, in some manner to intrude his own mind, heart and will into the process. Which is of course only to say that every man short of perfection is to that extent unable to think, feel and act according to the Mind, Heart and Will which I AM expresses by His Sayings. Men can therefore cease to hinder "the Godly Motion" of the Spirit of His

[1] Hos. 13,2.

94

Sayings only as they perfect their ability to receive the Sayings, and above all to receive them direct from I AM.[1] Thus receiving, they begin to be raised to the stature of Jesus Who *had* the Words so perfectly that He *was* The Word incarnate. Then, as His true disciples, they are able to transmit the Spirit of the Sayings as He did.[2] Short of that point, dilution and distortion are inevitable.

With this ineluctable fact in mind, let us now glance at its main consequences. Since there is at present no historical evidence of any man in this world having so far attained the stature of Jesus, which He demonstrated by His full manifestation of the Glory of the infinite Reality, it follows that the dilution of the Sayings of I AM begins at the point where they are elaborated in scriptures, sacramental systems and codes of Divine laws. No one can have known this better than the spiritual giants who did this work of elaboration. We cannot imagine, say, the authors of the Psalms or Epistles claiming the same importance for their work as for the Sayings of I AM which formed its whole ground and inspiration. Indeed, it was the clear distinction they drew between His Spirit and their own that enabled them to receive His inspiration.

But the more inspired their work was, and therefore the more inspiring, the more liable spiritually lesser men were to equate it with the Sayings it is built upon. So arose the virtual worship of the Bible, the Sacraments and the Divine Laws, leading to such views as fundamentalism, that Grace may be received without faith, that good works can alone bring about spiritual growth, and so on. Such virtual worship is idolatry, and as such cuts the idolater off from the fulness of inspiration which comes from the Sayings of I AM that *are* Spirit. His *own* Words alone perfectly utter the Truth of His Mind, the Beauty of His Heart, and the Goodness of His Will.

This initial step led to the next one, farther astray, in which the Spirit of the Sayings became still more diluted. The propagation of the scriptures, sacraments and Divine laws necessarily calls for commentaries, theologies, philosophies. Whoever recognised them in their proper role as aids, of course found them to point to the Spirit of the Sayings and to the Truth, Beauty and Goodness

[1] Collect for Lent 1.
[2] Jn. 8,31.

they represent. But the more enlightening these aids were, the more liable they were to be equated with the scriptures, sacraments and laws themselves, and to that extent with the Sayings upon which they rest. Every generation seems to regard itself richer in inspired sages, prophets and saints than posterity admits. So the traditions of men, in the language of I AM incarnate, make "the Word of God of none effect".[1] And so the Spirit of His Words becomes ever more diluted by and through men who stray into progressively cruder idolatry.

From this point the angle of departure from the Spirit of the Sayings grows more acute, as of sheep going ever further astray.[2] The commentaries, theologies, philosophies necessarily call for application to practical life on earth. The a priori approach calls forth its a posteriori counterpart. The resulting emphasis on the corporeal aspect of the Reality equally necessarily demands the development of non-spiritual sciences, secular arts and pragmatic ethical systems. Whoever recognises their spiritual origin and purpose finds them redolent of the Spirit of the Sayings, and sees them as reflections of the Truth, Beauty and Goodness of the Reality in its spiritual aspect. But whoever puts these reflections in the place of their spiritual original, so that they represent to him the Holy Spirit, goes wholly astray. He falls into the most crude idolatry of all. Since these reflections are all concerned with the corporeal aspect of the Reality, such idolatry severs his contact with the prior spiritual one. And as always, the more ably these reflections are worked out, the more liable he is to accept them as full expressions of Truth, Beauty and Goodness. Here the Holy Spirit of the Sayings becomes diluted to the point of distortion, a caricature in which a part is put in the place of the whole.

However widespread this progressive departure from the Spirit of the Sayings may be, it cannot be universal. If it were, man would lose all possibility of spiritual growth and become unable to fulfil the purpose of his creation. Collective man is preserved from wholly departing from the Spirit of the Sayings for the same reason that the individual man's True Self is preserved in its essential purity whilst falling into subjection to the corporeal realm. Therefore at each stage in the progressive departure a certain number of men

[1] Mk. 7,13.
[2] Ps. 119,176.

are enabled to retain the Spirit of the Sayings sufficiently to prevent it being wholly lost.[1] In a sense, this "faithful remnant" in human society corresponds with the True Self in the individual man after his fall.

As the story of Abraham pleading for Sodom and Gomorrah suggests, the remnant necessary to safeguard man's spiritual growth appears to be very small.[2] Nevertheless, the varying rate of human progress suggests that, when the remnant falls below a certain level in quantity and quality, the spiritual growth of mankind in general slows to very near a standstill. When the main body of human society loses touch with the spiritual Reality and recognises only its corporeal counterpart as real, the infinite Reality ceases to have any meaning at all. Deprived of the ultimate Unity underlying all knowable things, the hitherto coherent and generally accepted threefold structure of the Reality disintegrates into mutually exclusive splinters. The "faithful remnant", dragging a spiritually anaemic tail, withdraws defensively upon an exclusively religious standpoint. Their spiritually most blind and therefore most convinced opponents aggressively adopt an exclusively secular position. The sceptical fringe in both the opposing camps rather hesitatingly drift towards the compromise of some partitive form of humanism.[3]

Following the disintegration of the threefold scheme of the Reality, *each* of the three main standpoints splits in its turn. The mind seeking Truth becomes separated from the heart feeling after Beauty and from the will pursuing Goodness. Thus the gaps tend to widen between men of theology, prayer and good works; between scientists, artists and politicians; between philosophers, psychologists and moralists; and so on. The leaders in these disciplines probably escape being imprisoned in their own field, and preserve some liberality of outlook. But those who are led drift helplessly into seeking to know "more and more about less and less", their view of the Reality becoming increasingly fragmentary and superficial. Since they tend to reduce all knowledge to its most practical aspects, sooner or later their whole thinking, feeling and activity comes to be guided solely by technology, pop art and fleeting convention.

[1] Rom. 11,1-4.
[2] Gen. 18,23-33.
[3] Which we have called the specifically humanist approach and which in the twentieth century is sometimes called "scientific humanism".

97

In the degree that the masses are self-conscious, they necessarily determine the structure of the society of which they form the majority. The civilisation they build therefore tends to be largely materialistic, profane and pragmatic. It is the antithesis of the City of God. In such a civilisation, which is as unfavourable to spiritual birth as deformity in an organism is to its powers of reproduction, the ultimate purpose of human existence is incomprehensible. No lesser purpose can be fully satisfying, least of all the fleeting aims offered by such a civilisation. In other words, it offers its members the greatest of all miseries, a meaningless existence.

[5]

We end this chapter by touching on the third strand in the dialectical pattern of man's spiritual growth. Here we shall see the profit man derives from his suffering due to a virtual standstill in his spiritual growth.

We saw that the failures to receive and transmit the Spirit of I AM given through His Words resulted in their progressive dilution. From the Sayings themselves we thus traced the emergence of the scriptures for the instruction of man's mind; of the sacraments for the vitalisation of his heart; of the commandments for the regulation of his will. These dilutions led to others. The scriptures bred theologies and philosophies; the sacraments bred other forms of devotion and the sacred arts; the commandments bred the moral laws and the legal codes. From this point further dilutions led to loss of contact with the spiritual Reality and, by largely focussing attention on the corporeal Reality, turned the dilutions into actual distortions of the Spirit given through the Words. The philosophies thus led on to non-spiritual sciences; the sacred arts to the secular arts and crafts; the legal codes to rules and conventions.

From the *exclusively* spiritual standpoint the process we have indicated certainly represents dilution and distortion. But it is clear that from the *exclusively* corporeal standpoint the process represents an immense proliferation of human thinking, feeling and activity, though at the cost of corresponding fragmentation of all three. As always, the process is fully intelligible only from the *all-inclusive* standpoint of I AM, which reconciles all opposites and contradictions.

From this standpoint the process is seen to be the creation of vast new areas in the corporeal realm for the reception of His Holy Spirit. We see a mass of raw material newly formed, soil in which His Words will be sown and bear fruit in wider areas of His incarnation.[1] The process is thus an indispensable prelude to a harvest which "truly is plenteous".[2]

This becomes still clearer when we view the process from the standpoint of the Many Selves, in terms of human experience, dealt with in the previous chapter. We saw then that, like the Prodigal Son, they must depart from the Truth, Beauty and Godness of their Archetype in order to re-discover these supreme values and thereby to possess them as their own. Having considered the process in more detail in the present chapter, we now see that their departure also enables them to possess these values in greater measure than was otherwise possible. The dilution and distortion of the Spirit of the Words whereby I AM expresses His Truth, Beauty and Goodness has been accompanied by an increase in self-consciousness, in the area of human subjection to the corporeal realm, and in consequent human suffering. But this has correspondingly increased the possibility of man's all-consciousness, the area in which he can (by serving) rule the corporeal realm, and the occasions of his suffering being fulfilled in joy.

The vast majority of men must suffer the frustration which is due to their thinking, feeling and activity being guided by nothing more spiritual than technology, pop art and fleeting convention, imagining these to represent the fulness of Truth, Beauty and Goodness. For this suffering alone can awaken them to their delusion. Only then can they transform the technology, pop art and conventions they have created, according to their re-discovered archetypal values. This is the pattern of their laborious transformation of the jungle of nature into the City and Temple of God. Their suffering meanwhile is the price they pay in the course of carrying out their creative work, to be fulfilled in joy.

From the all-inclusive standpoint of The SELF the process we have indicated is, in the last analysis, the pattern of "the increase of His Government" in the corporeal realm. Ultimately, it is the

---

[1] Mk. 4,8; Jn. 15,7 & 8.
[2] Mat. 9,37.

pattern of His manifestation, through the endless multitude and diversity of Selves, of the Glory of God in corporeal terms. Their weakness and suffering in the course of fulfilling the purpose of their creation is therefore no less His than their final fulfilment in power and joy. "MY Power", He therefore declares, "is made perfect in weakness".[1]

If the reader accepts our view of the opportunities that lie open to mankind, he will have to make a decision. Is he prepared, with the aid of Bible, Sacraments and Commandments, or their counterpart in other traditions, for the costly and enduring effort of receiving the Words of The Word of God directly from Him as He eternally utters them? Man cannot *directly* receive the inspiration of His Holy Spirit except through His Words. Only then can he hope to *have* the Words as Jesus did. And only then can he hope to *be* their sum, the Incarnate Word, as Jesus was, and so fulfil the purpose of corporeal human existence.

The next part of this book is intended for those who, having this hope, are prepared to purify themselves accordingly.[2] The exercises are set out there in terms of a priest's work. Once the principles they are based on are properly grasped, they can be translated into the terms of other work. This will have to be done, if *all* work is to become *divinely* inspired. But it can probably only be done by those who know any particular work from inside.

[1] 2 Cor. 12,9 RV.
[2] 1 Jn. 3,3.

100

PART II

Chapter 6

The Embodiment of Holiness

[1]

If the ultimate purpose of human existence is to embody The
Word in terms of endless multitude and diversity, and yet in that
harmonious unity which alone truly represents His SELF, it is
obvious that our whole life in this world and elsewhere must sooner
or later become one uninterrupted exercise in the supreme art of
receiving His Words, by which He becomes flesh in us. But we
shall never even begin to do this consciously in the hurly-burly of daily
life, unless we first train ourselves for it in the sheltered conditions
of retreats, quiet days and, above all, in daily periods of quiet.
So a soldier trains himself in peacetime manoeuvres for the conditions of war. And the more realistic the manoeuvres are, the
better they serve their purpose. The exercises that follow are
intended to be such manoeuvres, and they may very simply be
adapted for use in retreats lasting several days, single days, or daily
periods.

Since the Words we are to receive are aspects of The Word
Himself, it is obviously necessary to select them from the Scriptures
with the utmost care, in order to fit our stage of spiritual growth.
They must be as significant, as full of meaning as possible for that
stage, and they must be selected in the sequence best suited to that
stage. To discuss the question of selection in any detail would
side-track us into theory. It is enough to say here that whoever
has found Part I of this book significant, will probably in some
measure be ready to receive the Sayings we have selected here. Both
the Sayings and their sequence rest on the scheme of Divine self-
expression, or self-unfoldment, represented by the symbol on the
flyleaf and set out in Part I.

The better we understand that we are created to *fulfill* the self-
expressive unfoldment of I AM, the more we shall hope to discover

Him *from the very moment* He appears out of the unconscious depths of our self. Our whole fruitfulness depends upon how deeply we know all He does to create us as the branches which unfold the Vine of His SELF.[1] The very first of all the Sayings we should try to receive must therefore be one that signifies the all-transcending yet all-comprehending Unity of God prior to His self-unfolding procession.

Strictly, God in His Unity, as the Infinite ONE, is beyond all knowledge but that of I AM.[2] But unless we reach upwards and inwards and *feel after* His Unity hidden in the "cloud of unknowing", His procession out of it will be without significance for us.[3] We shall miss the First Moment of His self-unfoldment, as a sluggard misses the first flash of the rising sun, and our view of all that follows will be stunted. More exactly, we shall miss the first facet of I AM as He comes forth from the infinite Unity of God, His Will, and thus never appreciate His Loving Intention.

The Bible is of course very rich in Sayings which signify the all-transcending yet all-comprehending Unity of God. None is more significant than the following. "I AM God . . . the Holy One in the midst of thee".[4] It confronts us from the start with the fact of the Infinite ONE's presence in us through His I AM. It also reminds us from the start of His truest Name. Every other tends to evoke an external image of Him, putting Him outside our self, as an object. His truest Name points to the presence of His SELF *within* our self. He is beyond our fallen self, as the Supreme SELF Who is also our True Self. He is objectively present to us, but on the subjective side of us as the Supreme Subject, I AM. If our own self is to be assimilated with His SELF, it will therefore be more than ever important to call Him by His truest Name.

Our reception of the Saying must begin in our mind, as we saw in the previous chapter. And for this we have to make our mind as receptive as possible. One practical way is to attune our mind to the Saying by recalling its deepest significance for us. We must not allow ourselves to drift off into theologising. There are many other occasions for this. Here it would over-stimulate our own

---

[1] Jn. 15,5.
[2] Mat. 11,27.
[3] Ex. 19,9.
[4] Hos. 11,9.

thoughts and obscure the Divine Thought uttered by the Saying. What we must learn to do here is to marshal what theological knowledge we possess into the most profound yet succinct summary we can. So we begin to attune our mind to the Mind of I AM as He eternally utters the Saying. The "formula" set out at the beginning of chapter 5 is invaluable as a basis for this summary.[1]

We have already touched on His immanence "in the midst of us". What does He mean when He declares Himself to be the Holy One? However inexhaustible this may be, He must here be speaking of Himself as the infinite Source, Ground and Goal of all that is knowable. "Of Him, and through Him, and unto Him are all things", in S. Paul's language.[2] Since all that ever has been, is, or will be knowable issues from Him, depends upon Him, and returns into Him, He contains all things, in the highest sense. He is thus the One Whole, the Whole One, the Holy One in the Greek sense of the term as derived from *holos*. Nothing could possibly be outside or beyond Him in any possible sense.

The term Holiness has another meaning, and we owe this to Hebrew insight. To the Hebrew, God's Holiness especially signifies His *separateness* or *otherness* from all else. Let us call this His exempt transcendence. Although He contains all things whatsoever, yet He is eternally above, beyond and exempt from all that proceeds from Him, rests upon Him, and returns into Him.

We need only touch on one further meaning of the term Holiness. This is commonly understood as moral or spiritual perfection, or both. Let us take this to mean the Holy One's perfection in every conceivable sense, His Absolute Perfection. And let us understand this to mean, at the very least, that there is absolutely no *lack* in Him. Nothing is un-manifested, un-expressed, not yet unfolded in Him. All that *can* be already *is* in Him.

Put together, these three meanings give us as rich a theological summary of Holiness as we need in order to attune our mind to the Saying we are about to receive. And let us remember again that He, Who is the Holy One in this tremendous triple significance, declares His SELF to be in the depth of each one of us. Having thus lifted up our mind to I AM, we take the next step in making

[1] Page 82.
[2] Rom. 11,36 RV.

ourselves as receptive as possible to the Saying. We deliberately stop all further thinking and still our mind so that it may be filled with nothing but the Saying itself. At the same time we adopt the posture which is most conducive to stillness: physical, mental and otherwise.

The physiological and psychological advantages of the most suitable posture for contemplation are too well known to be gone into here. We need only recall its essentials. These are to sit upright, the head and backbone in as straight a line as possible without strain, the hands resting on the knees or thighs, both feet on the ground The spiritual significance of this posture is perhaps less well known than its other advantages. This posture, which is clearly illustrated in representations of some of the Pharaohs, has been consciously or unconsciously selected by many great painters as best signifying the Lord of Heaven and Earth. Nothing is more evocative of the indwelling presence of the Holy One as He fills Heaven, His Throne, and Earth, His Footstool.[1] His Kingdom, His Sovereignty, is within us.[2]

Having adopted this most significant posture, we go on to deepen our stillness and receptivity by deliberately relaxing as far as possible. We take a few deep breaths, let our full weight rest on our chair, and relax any muscular tensions we detect. Lastly, in order to sharpen our concentration, we fix our whole attention on three in- and out-going breaths. This act of concentration on our breathing may be used to symbolise our coming effort to breathe in the Holy Breath of I AM by means of His Words. Then we turn our attention wholly from our self, face the abyss of unconsciousness beyond our self, and let nothing but the Saying dwell in us as richly as we can, in S. Paul's language.[3] In order to fill our whole mind with the Saying, we mentally repeat it just fast enough to exclude everything but the Divine Thought it represents.

"I AM God . . . the Holy One in the midst of thee".

We know that I AM is hidden in that abyss of unconsciousness beyond our self, so aptly called the "cloud of unknowing". It stretches beyond the summit of our self, hiding the heights of All-

---

[1] Isa. 66,1; Jer. 23,24.
[2] Lk. 17,21.
[3] Col. 3,16.

consciousness which the Bible calls "the Hill of the Lord".[1] In being thus turned inwards, expectantly listening to the Saying coming to us out of the "cloud", it is as though we were poised on our toes, with our arms stretched out, reaching upwards to the utmost of our strength. So our concentrated attention reaches inwards to meet I AM, Who by His Saying comes to us in the "thick cloud" that hides Him.[2]

[2]

After a few seconds the keen point of our concentration tends to become blunted, and our own thoughts begin to intrude on our mental repetition of the Saying. We may, for instance, find ourselves pondering the implications of our own un-holiness. We may recognise its fruits in the form of our failings, sufferings, burdens. From here we may pass to irrelevancies, and end by thinking utter rubbish. As soon as we let go of the Saying, allowing our fallen self to re-assert itself, our thoughts naturally tend downwards in quality, as water natuarally flows downhill. Suddenly realising how far they have strayed from the Divine Thought we are trying to hold in mind, we are tempted to throw the distraction out impatiently. But this only increases its distracting effect. If it cannot be gently extruded, by tranquilly repeating the Saying, it is best dealt with on the principle of giving it rope to hang itself by, for instance as follows.

Breaking off our mental repetition of the Saying, we examine the distracting thought objectively, as though it were someone else's. However exalted it is, it is not that of I AM. It thereby reminds us of the abysmal distinction between itself and the Divine Thought, and indeed between our whole fallen self and The SELF in the midst of us. So the distracting thought pin-points our fallen self, which obstructs I AM in us as the moon does the sun's light in an eclipse, and thereby keeps us from the supreme joy of fulfilling the purpose of our existence. So the distracting thought is used to eliminate itself and lead us back to the Saying.

[1] Ps. 24,3.
[2] Ex. 19,9.

The same principle can be applied to a particular kind of distraction with much greater profit. The thoughts that usually distract us most persistently are not the most exalted nor the most trivial ones, which are merely due to weak concentration, but those that concern our various burdens in life. If a persistent distraction is found to be emotionally charged, no further attempt should be made to extrude it. This would obviously be psychologically unsound. It would also be spiritually unsound in depriving us of an opportunity to use the distraction to our profit, say, as follows.

As soon as we recognise the *painful* content of the distraction, we make this remind us, not only of our fallen self which has bred it, but of the call of I AM to all sufferers to come to Him for rest. "Come unto ME, all ye that labour and are heavy laden, and I will give you rest".[1] We then try to respond to the call as completely as possible. We turn to I AM within us *with* our burden. This encourages us to examine the burden as objectively as possible, to face it without shrinking, and to accept it as our own. Until we have accepted it, we cannot truly come to I AM *with* it.

This is not always as easy to do as it sounds. If the burden is really painful, or still more so if it is shameful, we may well have formed the habit of minimising or disguising it. (If we deny its existence altogether, we are hardly ready yet for these exercises). A determined effort may then be necessary to concentrate on it, as though grasping a snake by its neck, and drag it out of the semi-conscious regions of the mind in order to face it squarely. It may help us to face and to accept it as though inwardly talking to it. "There you are", one might say to it, "my hatred of some person; my fear of death; my fear of the death of someone I love . . . "

Having in some such way faced and accepted the burden, we trace it to the weakness, failure, sin in us from which it stems. Whatever weaknesses may generate these burdens, faithlessness must be among them, and the whole fallen state of our self at the bottom of them all. Here is the root cause of all suffering, our own and that of all other human beings. There can be no final release from suffering until the cause of all suffering has been destroyed. The destruction of our fallen self must be endured before we can be free of suffering. Suffering can only be overcome by suffering. With these ineluctable

[1] Mat. 11,28.

facts in mind, we try to acknowledge without reserve, not only the particular sin responsible for our burden, but also the fallen state of our whole self responsible for our suffering and for that of others. Then we renounce our sin, and our fallen self, as resolutely as we can, as though throwing it off. By thus making it objective, we discriminate ever more clearly between our fallen self to be "put off" and our True Self to be "put on", in S. Paul's terms. So our heaviest burdens can be made not only to lead us back to the Saying we have strayed from, but to break down our natural resistance to learn from I AM, to take His Yoke upon us, by receiving the Spirit of His Saying.[1]

We must of course beware of getting lost in excessive introspection in the course of such self-examination, for this would defeat our whole purpose here. No more than two minutes should be allowed from the time we respond to the call of I AM, to come to Him with our burdens, to the time we return to the Saying we are mentally repeating. If this period is too short for the searching self-examination that is necessary, as it undoubtedly will be at first, it must be gone through at greater length elsewhere. As our self-knowledge increases, and with it the distinction between our fallen and our True Self grows clearer, our resolution to "deny" what we are for the sake of what we hope to be grows stronger.[2] Practice will enable us to make this denial and take the vital step from mortality into immortality, not in minutes, but in seconds, and even less.[3]

As we return to the mental repetition of the Saying, purged in the degree that we have genuinely denied, renounced our fallen self, our mind becomes correspondingly fitter to grasp its tremendous significance. "I AM God . . . the Holy One in the midst of thee". This increased awareness itself compels increasing attention to the Saying. As we succeed in letting it dwell in us, it draws us to Him Who utters it out of the "cloud of unknowing" beyond the summit of our self. Or conversely, by His Saying He comes into our self, as light into darkness.[4] "Lo", He declares, "I come to thee in a thick cloud".[5]

[1] Mat. 11,29.
[2] Mk. 8,34.
[3] Jn. 5,24.
[4] Eph. 5,14.
[5] Ex. 19,9.

As our mind grasps His presence in the midst of us, as though revealed by His Voice, so the abysmal distinction between our fallen self and His SELF grows ever sharper. According to His promise, our fallen self begins to repel us. "Ye shall know that I AM the Lord", He declares", and ye shall loathe yourselves".[1] In the light of His SELF, our fallen self stands out as a tomb in which our True Self lies buried. I AM, by His Saying uttered from within the tomb, gives us the power to break out. Another promise becomes fulfilled for us. "I will open your graves", He says, "and cause you to come up out of your graves".[2] So we receive strength to endure the cross for the joy that is set before us.[3]

"I AM God . . . the Holy One in the midst of thee". As we settle down to the mental repetition of the Saying, letting it dwell in us ever more richly, so to that extent the mind of our repellent fallen self gives way to the Mind of I AM. And to that extent, if only for a momentary flash, we *know* even as we, and all other things, are known.[4] This is the measure of our awakening to our True Self.

"I AM God . . . the Holy One in the midst of thee".
Ten to fifteen minutes' silence.

[3]

Having done our best to receive the Saying in the mind, we prepare for the next Silence in which we shall try to taste the feeling that is alive in it. To that extent we shall receive the Saying in the heart. We shall understand the Idea uttered by the Saying only in so far as we share in that feeling, only in so far as we know what it *feels like* to be the Holy One. We must therefore prepare for the second Silence by attuning our heart to the Saying, as we previously attuned our mind.

We did this by summing up our knowledge of Holiness in terms of theology. The heart may be attuned by summing up our knowledge in terms of experience. Since such knowledge is far subtler

[1] Ezek. 20,42 & 43.
[2] Ezek. 37,12.
[3] Heb. 12,2.
[4] 1 Cor. 13,12.

than intellectual knowledge, this summing up needs more skill and discipline. If we had to beware of getting side-tracked into theological speculations before, we now have to beware of being carried away by exalted feelings. It is, for instance, safer not to recall any particularly vivid spiritual experiences we have had. However impressive they may have been, there is nothing to guarantee their objective truth. There is certainly nothing to guarantee that they were experiences of Holiness. We need for our recollection some set of experiences which are independent of our own feelings and which objectively point us towards what it must feel like to be the Holy One. Our priestly work seems to offer us what we need.

The Epistle to the Hebrews suggests that certain priestly acts were regarded as corporeal representations of acts performed by The Christ in the spiritual realm.[1] The profound significance of the Holy Eucharist is widely held to include the sacrifice ceaselessly performed by The Christ in that realm. The administration of any Sacrament must involve some direct link between acts in the spiritual and corporeal realms. In performing his priestly acts, a priest usually treats them as means of worship, not experience. We shall therefore have to consider them as means of experience for our purposes now, after choosing one that suits our particular requirement. We choose the act of pronouncing the Blessing upon the congregation in the Name of God. It is well suited to point objectively towards what it may feel like to be the Holy One.

At first sight this may seem a rather brief act to choose, involving a colourless experience. This very quality, however, gives it relative immunity from subjective interference from the fallen self, at any rate until we are more practised in being taught by our priestly work in this manner. At the moment that the priest gives the Blessing he is least conscious of his own personality or that of the congregation. He speaks in the Name of God, as the mouthpiece of the Holy One. It is particularly interesting to note what he actually does in giving the Blessing. In the language of the Bible, he at that moment puts the Name of God upon the people.[2] Since the Name of God is I AM, he at that moment projects the Holy selfhood of God upon the selves composing the congregation. Let

---

[1] Heb. 8,5.
[2] Num. 6,23-27.

us recall the actual circumstances of the priest at the altar at that moment.

As he stands at the altar, he includes all the congregation in the Blessing he mediates, while they depend entirely upon him for all that the Blessing signifies. At that moment, therefore, his situation points to the Holiness of God in the sense of all-inclusiveness. Yet he stands at the altar beyond the congregation, is quite separate from them, and is not affected by them. This points towards the Holiness of God in the sense of His exempt transcendence. Lastly, the Blessing signifies the outpouring of all the unsearchable riches of Divine selfhood, whereby all who receive them are united with each other and their Source. This points towards Holiness in the sense of Perfection. At that moment the whole situation the priest is in thus conspires to give him an objectively true pointer towards what it may feel like to be the Holy One. And it is objectively true precisely because he is not at that moment concerned with the experience.

As we now meditate on the experience in this light, though never forgetting that it can do no more than point us towards the Divine Feeling of Holiness, which is ineffable, our heart becomes attuned to receive that Feeling as enshrined in the Saying. So we become ready for the next Silence. Here we shall mentally repeat the Saying as before, but now try to *taste* the Divine Feeling that lives in it. So its theological meaning will "come alive" for us. By withdrawing attention from our own feelings and looking to the Saying to give us the Divine Feeling enshrined in it, we are as little open to subjective intrusions as we are when giving the Blessing. We therefore deliberately put away, not only our own thoughts as before, but our own feelings, including those just reflected upon in attuning our heart.

"I AM God . . . the Holy One in the midst of thee".

Ten to fifteen minutes' silence.

[4]

Having done our best to receive the Saying, first in the mind, then in the heart, we now prepare for the third and last Silence of this exercise. Here we shall try to receive the Saying in our will, that is to say, try to express it by our will. More exactly still, we shall try to use our will to let the Saying possess our will and express itself through us. So the Saying, having informed our mind and then come to life in our heart, now begins to work in us.[1] To that extent it does the Will of the Holy One in us "as in Heaven, so on Earth".[2] For to that extent the Holy Spirit of His Words inspires us and He is flesh in us.

Since we are at present engaged in an excercise, we can of course only practise in the imagination this surrender of our will to be used by the Saying. We can practise it by imagining any situation in which our fallen self would be likely to act in an un-holy manner. It is best not to imagine any particularly dramatic situation. For this might not only stimulate our fallen self's will beyond our power to surrender to the Divine Will, but be so unrealistic as to reduce the exercise to one of fancy rather than spiritual growth, thus calling a sense of humour to our aid rather than anything else. We need some trivial situation in which we are naturally inclined to feel small, weak, inadequate and therefore tempted to assert ourselves with un-holy violence, but which can nevertheless become critical for our work as parish priests.

The imagined situation we choose, probably familiar to most of us in some form, is one which involves some interference with our responsibility as parish priests. Since we are concerned here with feelings leading to actions, and will have to re-experience those feelings in the course of the exercise, the situation cannot be merely indicated in the abstract but will have to be described with some fairly evocative detail. At first sight these feelings may appear rather primitive for a civilised person, especially a priest. If so, we may remember that every normal human being not yet a saint possesses these feelings, however much he may disguise or inhibit them, or however deep in his subconsciousness they may be buried. The greater his self-knowledge is, the more clearly he is aware of them at work in him. Hence he may be aware of feelings which in others are below the threshold of consciousness. He does not shrink from this, however, if he realises that *every* natural feeling must be uncovered to its sub-human roots before it can be transformed into its supra-natural archetype in the course of his purification.

[1] 1 Thes. 2,13.
[2] Mat. 6,10 RV.

111

Let us imagine a day on which we are particularly heavily engaged, when without prior warning one of our most dominating church-people who has just been elected warden appears at the door and wishes to see us at once. He has a plan for improving the Sunday Services. He wishes the Epistle to be omitted from the Liturgy. (An authentic case). In his view, it is usually incomprehensible and prolongs the Service to no purpose. Clearly he assumes that the conduct of the Services is at least as much the warden's responsibility as the priest's.

The position is plain. If we are not to surrender our responsibility for the spiritual welfare of the parish to the warden, which is of course out of the question, we must make clear to him that his assumption is mistaken. The impulse at once stirs in our fallen self to assert ourselves with irony or plain anger. And the weaker it feels in face of a rather dominating opponent, the more violent the impulse tends to be.

This weakness, compensated for by violence, is the greatest contrast we need imagine here with the Divine Feeling of Divine Holiness, the Feeling of all-comprehending yet all-transcending Perfection. If we allow the weakness to manifest itself in something we say or do, this will be equally un-holy. Civilised habit prompts us to use our will to suppress anger in order to deal with our opponent calmly. If we suppress anger, however, this emotion will remain essentially unimpaired in us, ready to erupt again on another occasion, and we shall not gain an inch in spiritual growth. Moreover, by acting in a civilised manner alone, the act will be without spiritual power. We shall reject the warden's proposal, for instance, but leave him still in opposition. So instead of using our will in some such way, we must practise surrender to the Will of I AM as expressed by the Saying. To be precise, we must practise using our will to stop us doing anything *ourselves,* and instead use it to let the Saying work in us, so that we might thereby become a channel of the Divine Will.

Earlier on we likened our exercises to manoeuvres. The effectiveness of both largely depends upon their realism. We must therefore imagine the warden's challenge to our authority as parish priest as realistically as possible. The realism of manoeuvres particularly demands the use of the same weapons as in war. Hence we must prepare to meet the imagined challenge with the same weapon as we shall rely upon in a real situation. The weapon we have to learn to use, or more precisely, to be used by, is of course the Saying. Nothing could be more significant than S. Paul's description of "the Word of God" as the "Sword of the Spirit".[1] Or the description elsewhere of the Word as "sharper than any two-edged sword", that is, more effective than any corporeal action.[2] We shall now consider how to use the Sword of the Spirit in the situation we are imagining, and thereby attune our will to the Saying, and to the Will of the Holy One expressed therein, as we earlier attuned our heart and our mind.

Let us begin by imagining our interview with the warden as vividly as possible. Having dropped into our study armchair without an invitation, he argues his case in favour of omitting the Epistle from the Liturgy. Well before he has finished his exposition of his view, we feel the impulse rising in us to cut him short and tell him forcefully that, the priest being solely responsible for all Services in the parish, we are not prepared to discuss his proposal. As he continues his self-assured discourse, our self-assertive impulse becomes reinforced with anger, until we are about to arise in wrath.

This is the moment to meet our opponent, not with the natural weapon of anger, nor with the civilised weapon of irony, but with the spiritual one of the Saying. Let us clearly realise how to conduct this spiritual fight. Instead of using our will to suppress anger, or to disguise it with a civilised veneer, we must use it to fix our whole attention on the Saying. "I AM God . . . the Holy One in the midst of thee". If we can mentally repeat the Saying for even a few times in the teeth of anger, thereby turning from our fallen self, denying it, seeking to lose it, our previous experience of Holiness gained in the Silence before should be reawakened.[3] So the Spirit of the Words will begin to "direct and rule our hearts".[4] And so the Words will begin to work in us. As our anger is, not suppressed or disguised, but *washed away*, we shall cease to regard our visitor as an opponent.[5]

---

[1] Eph. 6,17.
[2] Heb. 4,12.
[3] Mat. 10,39.
[4] Collect for Trinity XIX.
[5] Prayer of Humble Access.

Our anger may possibly flare up again and interrupt the work of the Saying in us. This may be due simply to our concentration fading; but if not, it may be that the Divine Feeling alive in the Saying is reaching and washing away our anger at a less conscious level of our fallen self than hitherto, and in so doing making manifest what had previously been sub-conscious. The resurgent anger is then a welcome sign that our fallen self is being more radically purged than before. In either case, the interruption should be treated as a challenge to our will to keep our attention fixed on the Saying.

As we learn to surrender to the Saying, we begin to abide in I AM Who utters it. Or conversely, as we will ourselves to be possessed by the Saying, I AM begins to abide in us.[1] To that extent the Holy One becomes flesh in us by means of His Words, and dwells and walks in us.[2] As we thereby *rest* in His all-comprehending yet all-transcending Perfection, no longer trying to do anything ourselves, our opponent ceases to appear formidable to us.[3] His challenge to our authority shrinks correspondingly. There is no longer any cause for our anger, and it begins to give place to compassion and gentleness. So by the spiritual power of the Saying, the Sword of the Spirit, we overcome our opponent in the full sense. For being empowered to treat him kindly and gently, we not only cease to regard him as an opponent but enable him to cease regarding us as one too. It is immaterial in what words we reject his proposal. What matters is that we do it in a spirit and manner which stops him saying any more, simply because he has ceased to be our opponent.

Having imagined this situation in order to attune our will to the Saying and to determine the proper use of the Sword of the Spirit, we now prepare to practise its use in the last Silence of this exercise. Its most crucial point is obviously where the feeling of anger in us is exposed to, and replaced by, the Divine Feeling of Holiness enshrined in the Saying. For since action issues from feeling, it is at this point that we must practise willing ourselves to let the Saying work in us. As we now begin mentally repeating the Saying, we imagine ourselves in our study angrily facing the warden. However hard we may have found it to concentrate on the Saying in the two

[1] Jn. 15,4.
[2] 2 Cor. 6,16.
[3] Ex. 33,14.

previous Silences, we shall find it very much harder in this emotionally charged situation. This difficulty measures the strength of the anger which has to be washed out of us, and of our fallen self which has to be destroyed, before I AM can dwell and walk in us.

"I AM God . . . the Holy One in the midst of thee".

Ten to fifteen minutes' silence.

With this third and last Silence our present exercise in receiving the Saying, and to that extent *having* it, comes to an end. We are now in duty bound to thank I AM for the gift of His Holiness to us through the Saying. We are wise to give thanks for our own sake also. For our thanks to Him ever remind us of the objective presence of His SELF within the subjective depth of our fallen self. The more often we thank Him, the more clearly we learn to distinguish between these two extremes of selfhood within us.

Our final act in the exercise should be to offer to I AM all that we are, all that we have, and all that we do, in return for His gift of His SELF to us. Here too we are not only in duty bound to do so, but wise to do so for our own sake. For this constant offering of our whole self is one of the most direct ways of shedding the cause of all suffering, until there is nothing more left to offer.

[5]

The more complex any manoeuevre is, the more its details have to be practised before attempting the whole. Recruits learn "by numbers" what trained soldiers do as a single movement. Hence the exercise just completed was set out in three clear-cut sequential stages involving mind, heart and will in turn. For this is the order, let us remember, in which man most directly embodies The Word by means of His Words. These three stages should therefore be practised separately whenever practicable, such as in retreats or quiet days. But since spiritual growth is a living process, and since these three stages represent a division only for training purposes, the exercise should also be attempted as a whole every day. Here the three stages should as far as possible be combined, so that the last includes and fulfils the two preceding ones. For it is the last which is crucial to progress in the embodiment of the Saying. But as always, it is useless trying to run before being able to walk, and in jumping to any stage without the proper work in the preceding one merely causes some such distortion of the Saying as was mentioned in Chapter 5.[1] Therefore as soon as such a tendency is detected, we should at once return to the three stages separately.

Two daily Silences of ten minutes are about the minimum for any serious attempt to embody the Saying. A third Silence would increase the efficacy of the exercise by much more than this proportion. A fourth still more. For since we are concerned with a living not a mechanical process, the capacity of the fallen self to revive after each systematic denial we make of it shrinks with more than arithmetical progression. The awakening of the True Self of course advances at the same rate.

The amount of time and energy spent in the daily exercises will largely determine the number of days that should be spent in working for the embodiment of the Saying. The period should be long enough to enable us to receive some degree of Holiness not possessed hitherto, however small, yet not long enough to cause staleness. A very rough guide is a month. But the advice of one more experienced in these exercises is the best guide.

No one who realises the importance of this work will lack the time for these Silences. But he will have to be very well advanced if he never lacks the energy to endure the mental, emotional and above all the volitional effort they involve. It is well to remember that we actually move towards the fulfilment of the purpose of our existence in the degree that we tax our endurance to the limit.[2]

It remains for us to outline an essential extension of the daily practice of the exercise. Without this, however determined the daily practice may be, the three stages of the exercise will probably never be fully combined. This means that the exercises will never be applied in the trials of everyday life, for which we have trained ourselves by using the imagination. We shall be in the position of a soldier who faces his opponent in battle, unable to use his bayonet except "by numbers". This extension is thus really the fulfilment of the whole exercise. Its proper use will govern the number of days spent in trying to embody the Saying quite as much as the daily practice we have described.

[1] Page 93-96.
[2] Mat. 24,13.

116

This essential extension consists of the simple but difficult act of recalling the Saying as often as possible throughout the day. It is as though we constantly reached for the Sword of the Spirit, thereby growing "quicker on the draw" in case of need. The whole Saying may be found too cumbersome for these brief recollections; if so, it may be shortened, provided its essential meaning is not altered. This shortened version is then understood to represent the whole, as a hilt does the sword. The shortened version may also be regarded as a watchword which represents a fuller statement. Our present Saying may safely be shortened to the following watchword: "I AM . . . in thee".

Our recollection of the Saying is greatly helped if we write it carefully on a small card, with the watchword above it. This card can then be carried about as a tangible symbol of the Saying we aspire to embody. In that sense it assumes a sacramental significance. Furthermore, by carefully writing the Saying out in our own hand, we help to make it our own. It certainly is our True Self's own, and our True Self utters it beyond space, time and change, whether our fallen self knows it or not.

By far the most important of these momentary recollections of the watchword or Saying is as we fall asleep. For the Saying, and especially the Divine Feeling with which it is charged, continues to work in our subconsciousness throughout the night. Though not easy, once this has been learned and becomes habitual, the indwelling presence of I AM can become far more vivid in the act of losing consciousness than when fully awake. If sleep is the "little death", this fact has important implications too long to be gone into here. The next most important moment to recollect the Saying is as we awaken. For the day then begins in the light of the Saying. This makes it correspondingly easier to recall it at other moments in the day. So we become overshadowed by it, and surrender with increasing ease to its work in us. So we begin to approach the state of ceaseless prayer, and the point where we eternally abide in the Holy One, and He in us.[1]

---

[1] 1 Thes. 5,17; Jn. 15,4.

Chapter 7

The Embodiment of Divine Love

[1]

We have done our best to receive the Saying signifying the Holiness of I AM, and in that degree embody His all-inclusive yet all-transcending Perfection. So we are as fit as we can be at this stage of our spiritual growth for an attempt to embody the First Moment of His self-revealing, self-expressing, self-unfolding procession out of the hidden depth of His infinite Unity. And so, as we follow Him coming forth out of the cloud of unknowing in our own inner depth, beyond the summit of our own self, we may participate in that procession in the course of which He makes, upholds and fulfils all things visible and invisible. As we saw in Chapter 3, this First Moment reveals the first of the three facets of His I AM: His Creative Intention, His Loving Will, the Loving Goodness of His Will. It is this alone which ensures the perfect goodness of His Reality in process of manifestation, the knowable Reality of which His own SELF is the sum. And although His Holiness in its fulness is beyond all possible knowledge, we have had to "feel after" it because perfect Goodness of Will is only intelligible as the outcome of Holiness. Much as giving is only intelligible as the outcome of possessing.

As we prepare to consider this first facet of I AM, and its work in the First Moment of His creative procession, let us again remember that essentially this is not a process at all. The Will, Heart and Mind of I AM do not work successively. For He is beyond time. As the Chaldean Oracle significantly puts it, "The ONE spake, and *immediately* The THREE came forth . . ." We are obliged to consider what is accomplished by The ONE's Will, Heart and Mind (The THREE) in successive stages only because our own limitations as learners demand such an approach. At first that alone is how we can logically think, psychologically experience and practically express

118

these stages in our life. Here is another instance of our having to do "by numbers" in order to learn what I AM does simultaneously and timelessly.

The work accomplished by the Loving Good Will of I AM is set out in Chapter 3 and summed up in the "formula" in Chapter 5,[1] and all we need do here is to review its essence in order to marshal our theological knowledge on the subject, and select from the Bible the Saying which will signify it most fitly for our reception at this stage. The essential work of His Will stands out as soon as we recall what happens when The ONE speaks and The THREE come forth. In the act of speaking, The ONE really breaks and gives away His ineffable infinite Unity for the sake of revealing, expressing, unfolding this as Triunity, I AM. The work of His Loving Goodness of Will is thus essentially self-sacrifice in its purest form of self-breaking and giving away.

We next recall that there is nothing outside, beyond, or beside I AM to call forth this sacrificial act. It springs from nothing whatever but the Nature, the Essence, the Being of His SELF. His "property is always to have mercy", as the Prayer of Humble Access puts it. Which is also why S. John calls Him Love, as we have seen. He breaks and gives away His SELF in sacrificial Love purely for the sake of making His Infinity knowable, with all the inexhaustible consequences that follow. It is His Loving Good Will to spend His SELF to the uttermost in the fulness of self-revelation, self-expression, self-unfoldment. His Love, without as yet any object to call forth this sacrifice of His whole SELF, without as yet any beloved, is thus perfectly disinterested. His Love is its own self-sufficient cause, the essence of causality, and the supreme pattern of all purely self-expressive causation.

This brief review helps us to search the Bible for the Saying which most clearly signifies to us the Divinely sacrificial act of Loving Goodness of Will. As one would expect, the Bible is very rich in Sayings signifying Divine Love, Mercy, Kindness. We are wise to choose one for a start which signifies as clearly as possible the *sacrificial* aspect of the Loving Will, and therefore the perfect Goodness of the Will of I AM. Later on, when we are no longer likely to sentimentalise Divine Love, or conceive it in the natural terms of

---

[1] Pages 49 and 82 respectively.

desire, or otherwise distort its essence, we may choose other Sayings. No Saying fits our need better than the following: "I AM the Bread of Life . . . which I will give . . . for the life of the world".[1] A few comments may help us to marshal our knowledge of Divine Love and thereby attune our mind to receive the Saying.

The first concerns the significance of the Bread of Life as an attribute of I AM. In the Holy Eucharist the Bread of course signifies the Body or Flesh of The Christ. Let us now recall the still deeper significance of the Body or Flesh, mentioned in Chapter 5.[2] To the Jew of the time in which the Sacrament was instituted the flesh of a creature signified its essential nature or being, which when eaten became assimilated with his body. Hence he was forbidden to eat the flesh of certain creatures as unclean. In speaking of Himself as the Bread of Life, I AM incarnate therefore signifies His Divine Nature, Essence, Being. And we know that this underlies *all* Life, His own and all creation's.[3]

We next consider the intention signified by the Saying. I AM declares that He *will give* the Bread of Life, that is His Being, for the life of the world. We must beware of limiting the sense of these words to a mere promise regarding the future. Since His Being underlies *all* life, including His own, there can be no single moment in which He has not, does not, and will not give His Being for the life of the world. If He failed to do so, His own Being would cease to be Living, and all living things would instantly vanish. In their deeper significance His words must therefore be taken, not only as a promise, but as a declaration of His Will. He *wills* to *give* His Being for the life of the world. No Saying in the Bible brings out more vividly the sacrificial quality of the Loving Goodness of His Will.

The only other comment we need make here concerns the purpose to be fulfilled by this sacrificial act of His Loving Will. I AM breaks and gives away His Being for the life of the *world*. Here again we must beware of limiting the scope of His purpose. We must beware of parochialism in space, as we did just now of parochialism in time. Since no greater sacrifice is conceivable than the breaking and giving away of all Being, the effects thereby produced must be

[1] Jn. 6,48 & 51 RV.
[2] Page 83.
[3] Chapter 3 page 52.

the greatest conceivable too. The world which owes its life to the sacrifice of I AM cannot be limited to the planet we inhabit. All worlds throughout all ages which compose the everlasting Corporeal Universe would be inadequate as the effect of so tremendous a cause. The world of which I AM speaks in the Saying can mean nothing less than all that is in any degree alive, that is, for practical purposes, the whole knowable Reality. That means, for practical purposes, the Reality fulfilled in Man in its spiritual as well as in its corporeal aspects. All things whatsoever have life in their proper measure solely because I AM wills to break and give away His Being for their sake. His own Being is revealed as Living, indeed, only as the result of that sacrificial act.[1] All things whatsoever are therefore His, as He declares them to be, in the most inclusive sense.[2] They are His because He is their Source; His because He is their Ground; His because He is their Goal.

What we have said should suffice as a summary of the theological meaning of the Saying and help us to attune our mind for its reception. It is tempting to meditate further on its significance, but this might easily turn our mind *from* rather than *to* the Divine Mind we seek to put on by means of the Saying, and so we resolutely still our own thoughts in preparation for the first Silence of this exercise.

We adopt the proper bodily posture, relax any muscular tensions of which we are aware, and concentrate our attention on three in- and out-going breaths. Our physical need for air is symbolic of our spiritual need for the inspiration of His Words that are Spirit and Life. The air entering our lungs thus symbolises the Holy Breath of I AM coming into us as His spiritual kiss of life. This need for His life-giving inspiration reminds us that we are still separate from Him, not yet one with Him. And this in turn reminds us of His call to us and to all mankind to come unto, into, Him. "Come unto ME, all ye that labour and are heavy laden, and I will give you Rest".[3] As we come into Him and become at-one with Him, we partake of His eternal state of Changelessness, which is Rest in its highest sense.

---

[1] See Chapter 3 for the First and Second Movements of His creative procession.

[2] Jn. 16,15 RV.

[3] Mat. 11,28.

MY Body which is given for you".[1] Presently taking the Sacrament Without allowing ourselves to be involuntarily distracted by our burdens, as in the first exercise, we precede our Silence with the two-minute period devoted to a deliberate recollection of the heaviest of these burdens. The rest are relatively unimportant at the moment. We face up to it, if necessary dragging it from the half-conscious levels of the mind where habit has caused us to hide it, and firmly accept it as our own. We trace it to the sins that have bred it, and renounce them. Lastly, we renounce our whole fallen self of which these and all other sins are like the individual sores of a diseased body, and which of course give us pain.

But however clearly the mind accepts this link between our fallen self and all suffering, both its own and others', we may find this act of renunciation a little perfunctory. If so, we owe this to our heart's much slower acceptance of the link, with the result that the will is not seriously stirred to any genuine act of renunciation. With its heart and will lagging behind its mind, our fallen self remains obstreporously alive. To that extent it of course resists the renunciation that threatens its existence.

As always, there is no short cut to getting the heart to experience whatever the mind has accepted as true. We can only continue to dwell on this link, go on proving its truth by stressing the undeniable experience of our burdens. Only experience can bring home to the heart the fact that there can be no relief from these burdens except by continually renouncing the fallen self which is their cause. They will disappear only when it is destroyed. And it is only in the degree that it is destroyed, and our True Self released, that we can truly ease other people of their burdens. It may help to recall the *mortality* of the thing we are so reluctant to renounce. Not only is it condemned to *taste* the pain of death, but it is destined to be destroyed altogether. For it is essentially nothing but the sleeping state of the True Self. In this light, a reluctance to renounce the deathbound thing has no point whatever.

As we constantly re-experience the link between our burdens and our fallen self, the heart will come to accept the fact. Then the fallen self's mortality, its impermanence, will become a promise of release from the tomb which imprisons our True Self. So we become able to end our two-minute period of self-examination with a decreasingly perfunctory renunciation of our fallen self And so we become correspondingly fit to receive the Saying we have chosen to signify the sacrificial Love, the Loving Goodness of the Will of I AM. Resolutely now putting away all our own thoughts, even the most exalted, we begin mentally repeating the Saying.

"I AM the Bread of Life . . . which I will give . . . for the
life of the world".

Ten to fifteen minutes' silence.

[2]

The Silence over, we prepare for the next one by attuning the heart to assimilate the Divine Feeling with which the Saying is charged. In this coming Silence we shall try to experience something of the Loving Goodness of the Will of I AM, try to share in the feeling that must be His as He breaks and gives away His SELF for the life of the knowable Reality. We shall attune our heart by the same method as in the previous exercise. Having chosen some appropriate priestly act, we shall meditate on the experience which is implicit in its performance, and use this as a pointer towards the ineffable Divine Feeling.

The most appropriate act is obviously the celebration of the Holy Communion, and particularly the actual consecration and administration of the bread, which signifies the Flesh or Body of The Christ, which in turn signifies the Essence or Being of I AM.

The first feature of the Celebration to be noticed in this regard is the care taken by the priest to ensure that the supply of bread exceeds any possible need for it. We are concerned here with the theological significance of this, of course, and not with the practical difficulty of running out. We may take the ample supply of bread to signify the fact that the Being of I AM, to be broken and given away, exceeds all the effects that can possibly flow from His sacrificial act. He is greater than all He contains, for He is the knowable Source, Ground and Goal of all that ever was, is, or can be.

The next feature is the consecration of the bread and its presentation to the congregation. In breaking the bread, the priest utters the words by which I AM incarnate instituted the Sacrament. "This is

[1] Lk. 22,19.

123

from the altar, he shows it to the congregation. These two related acts may be taken to signify the First Moment of the creative procession of I AM from the unknowable depth of His Unity. Here is the first revealing flash of His self-unfoldment in which He breaks His hidden Unity into His spiritually knowable Triunity, and by this supremely sacrificial act shows forth the Loving Goodness of His Will.

The next feature is the administration of the bread. The priest distributes to the communicants, not shapeless fragments of the broken bread, but cubes of about the same shape as the loaf they come from. This correspondence between the all-containing fontal whole and the lesser wholes emanating from it is clearer and more exact where circular wafers are used. The celebrant breaks the great circle of the priest's wafer, but what he distributes to the communicants are not its fragments but the perfect lesser circles of the people's wafers. Thus, though the great whole is broken *for the sake* of being given away, that which is actually *given away* is a series of perfect counterparts of the all-inclusive source. So, in distributing the wafers to the communicants at the altar, the priest may be said to show forth the all-prolific creativity of the sacrificial self-breaking and giving away of I AM. Its first effect is the differentiation of His SELF into the endless multitude and diversity of Selves in the course of His sacrificial descent into corporeal manifestation. Its next effect is their being spiritually fed, upheld thereby. Its last effect is their gathering together again into one Body, in which each nevertheless retains his unique individuality, whereby The SELF is manifested in the outermost corporeal conditions of space, time and change. All this flows solely from the Loving Goodness of His Will, as he eternally breaks and gives away His SELF as the knowable Source, Ground and Goal of all things. And this all-prolific sacrificial act is vividly shown forth by the priest's distribution of the consecrated bread to the communicants at the altar rail.

There are many other features of the administration of the Sacrament whose significance we might ponder, but space allows us only one more. This is the fact that the priest gives the bread to all who come legitimately to receive it. Some of the hands that stretch out for it are delicate and fine. Others are coarse and misshapen. Some of their owners receive the Sacrament with greater reverence, that is understanding, than others. Some are known to him to be more

worthy to receive it than others. But he gives the circle of wholeness without distinction of feeling or gesture to all who stretch out
their hands. He gives it freely, willingly, without reserve. **It cannot**
be snatched from him, or forced from him. As he gives it, he repeats
the essence of the Saying which signifies the tremendous gift: "This
is MY Body which is given for you." In being given *for* them, the
Body is sacramentally given *to* them. So the priest enacts the perfect
disinterestedness of the Loving Goodness of Will in which I AM
breaks and gives away His Being for the life of the knowable Reality.

It is hard to imagine any priestly act which points more vividly
and surely towards the ineffable feeling enshrined in the Saying we are
attuning our heart to assimilate. The very words uttered in the
course of that act, in consecrating and administering the bread, signify
the feeling of perfect Loving Goodness of Will. The priest's whole
action at the altar, indeed, is a clear corporeal counterpart of that
which I AM does spiritually in the First Moment of His creative
procession from the hidden depth of His Infinite Unity.

As we ponder this act and its significance, which we are not
usually able to do in the course of performing it, we increasingly
appreciate its value in pointing us towards the ineffable Divine
Feeling involved in I AM breaking and giving away His SELF
for the life of the world. The act enables the priest to know something of what it means, not only to *receive* the Being of I AM as
any communicant may, but to *give* the Supreme Gift. By enhancing
his faith, this experience enables him to realise the indwelling presence
of I AM correspondingly clearly. So the extraordinary privilege
conferred on him by priesthood comes home to him again.

Having attuned our heart to assimilate the ineffable feeling with
which the Saying is charged, we now put away all the thoughts
and experiences that have helped us to do this, and once more
concentrate on the mental repetition of the Saying. We do so
exactly as in the previous Silence, but because our heart and not
only our mind is now attuned to the Saying we are able to assimilate
something of the feeling it enshrines. It alone can give us that
feeling, so that as we begin mentally repeating the Saying we are
particularly careful not to evoke any experience that may have come
to us as priests at the altar. "I AM the Bread of Life . . . which
I will give . . . for the life of the world".

Ten to fifteen minutes' silence.

[3]

In the degree that we have received the Saying in the heart and, by tasting something of the Divine Feeling it enshrines, and in that degree understood the Idea it signifies, we are fit to profit by the last Silence of the exercise. The Idea having "come to life" for us, as is sometimes significantly said, we are ready to train our will to let the Saying work in us. As the exercise in the previous chapter must have shown, this is its crucial stage, in which we begin to embody the Saying. As we carry the exercise into practical life, we begin to manifest something of the presence of I AM in us and begin to bear fruit, as He says.[1]

At the end of the previous exercise we introduced the need to go about in workaday life armed with a watchword to represent the whole Saying. Henceforward during the last Silence we shall practise using the watchword as well as the whole Saying, and be that much more trained to meet the difficulties of everyday life. Let us begin by noting its purpose on these occasions. This is to nip in the bud the gathering reaction of our fallen self to some stimulus, in order to let the whole Saying it represents dwell and work in us. Without this, the reaction may well gather such speed and power in us, like a fire in straw, that we are emotionally too strongly moved to concentrate on the Saying at all. The quicker we are by temperament to react to internal or external stimuli, therefore, the more necessary it is to practise the use of the watchword.

But this is necessary, even if we are temperamentally slow to react. For as our self-examination grows more effective, we expose hitherto subconscious levels of our fallen self to the sanctifying work of the Sayings. As our will becomes better trained to surrender to the Sayings to do their work in us, the threshold of consciousness sinks in us, with the result that we become aware of hitherto unsuspected primitive feeling active in us. Our fallen self, if left to its own devices, becomes more prone to rapidly changing moods, irrational urges, sudden impulses. We seem to peer down the dark well of the evolutionary process, of which our bodies and natural feelings are the product, and find a snake-pit at the bottom of our fallen self. This growing awareness of hitherto subconscious levels

[1] Jn. 15,4.

of our fallen human inheritance and its sub-human foundations is necessarily painful, sometimes alarming, and occasionally dangerous. The fallen self cannot be left to its own devices, as in the days before we set out to destroy it. The traditional warnings against embarking on contemplative exercises irresponsibly, unworthily or without experienced guidance are certainly cogent.

We begin our preparation for the last Silence by choosing a watch-word. Our Saying signifies the Loving Goodness of Will in which I AM breaks and gives away His SELF for the life of the knowable Reality. The essence of the whole Saying lies in the three words signifying His Will *to give*. So let our watchword be: "I will give". Having chosen it, let us at once make an explicit act of will to use it in place of our own will. Then we go on to imagine the situation in which we shall practise using both watchword and Saying, or rather letting ourselves be used by them.

We can do no better than carry on our imaginary spiritual contest with our dominating warden. As we shall see later, ultimately he exposes our own fallen state, so that the contest is essentially with our own fallen self. This continuity will not only save having to describe new situations in detail, but enable us to use our relationship with an external opponent as a study in spiritual growth. Without claiming to have dealt with him in the last interview in the Spirit of Holiness, let us assume that we did not fail as badly as we would have done without being armed with the Saying, the Sword of the Spirit. The situation has consequently changed. As a result of our last interview, our opponent now appears less formidable to us. We begin to appreciate something of the service he does us by pin-pointing some of our un-holy features, exposing them to purgation by the Saying, and thereby weakening our whole fallen self.[1]

Furthermore, he helps us to see these un-holy features in a positive light. We already know in theory, on theological grounds, that the purpose of falsity, ugliness and evil in the corporeal realm, and the consequent suffering, is to bring home to fallen mankind the reality of Truth, Beauty and Goodness. The purpose of Satan's existence is to accuse man of his sins, as the Bible illuminatingly puts it.[2] As we have already remarked, however, the heart is very much slower to accept the truth than the mind. Our experience of actually

[1] Jn. 15,3.
[2] Job 1,9; 2,4 & 5; Rev. 12,10.

beginning to see our opponent the warden, this minor embodiment of "our adversary the devil", as our accuser helps to bring this difficult piece of theology to life. We really begin to *understand* the purpose of sin and suffering in the imperfect parts of the corporeal realm. Finally, we recognise that the service which our opponent unconsciously renders us gives him at least as much pain as it does us. To him we no doubt also represent "the adversary the devil".[1] For all these reasons we now regard him with a good deal more kindness than before.

He for his part is bound to regard us in a different light too, having noted the change in us. Let us suppose for purposes of this exercise that he is a tough opponent. Rather taken aback by his failure to get his accustomed way in the interview previously described, and therefore less self-assured, he collects support among other church-people for his proposal to omit the Epistle from the Liturgy, and demands to bring a deputation to see us. He himself is no longer calmly superior, but is getting angry.

We imagine ourselves back in our study, and see a considerable group crowding in, obviously bent on more or less polite coercion. It is now our turn to be taken aback at being so heavily outnumbered. Our kindness towards our opponent evaporates in face of a more formidable challenge to our authority as parish priest, responsible for the spiritual welfare of the parish. The reaction of our fallen self, anger now reinforced by apprehension in face of numbers, is correspondingly stronger.

Let us imagine these feelings rising in us and stirring us to assert our authority. However we choose to do this, its essential effect must be to *take away* from our opponent the power of opposing us, if necessary to take away, remove, get rid of him altogether. We feel this impulse to *deprive* him which, when carried to its extreme becomes murderous. It is the very opposite of the Loving Goodness of Will in which I AM breaks and *gives away* His SELF for the life of the world.[2] This angry impulse to harm must breed evil as surely as the Loving Will of I AM to benefit must breed Goodness. Let us suppose that the way we choose to assert our authority is by demanding, with an abrupt gesture, who is ultimately responsible for the spiritual welfare of the parish: warden or priest?

[1] 1 Pet. 5,8; Mat. 18,7.
[2] 1 Jn. 3,15.

We imagine the indignant words rising to our lips. Now, before the feeling rises to the point of discharging itself in words and gestures, is the moment to recall the watchword, as though firmly gripping the Sword of the Spirit. "I will give". By its very brevity it catches our attention enough to remind us of the whole Saying it represents. "I AM the Bread of Life . . . which I will give . . . for the life of the world". We will ourselves to start mentally repeating the Saying. In the first moment or two it may be a "vain repetition", but if we persevere it should begin to possess our mind. Then the Feeling with which it is charged, passing down to our heart, begins to replace the angry impulse to make the indignant demand and gesture. So the Saying, given "free course" in us, begins to work in us. And so some measure of the Loving Good Will of I AM is done in us in the form of some appropriate phrase or gesture. We have to reject his proposal, of course, but we do so kindly and gently. Since we do this in the face of a more severe challenge than in the last exercise, it represents a correspondingly greater manifestation of spiritual strength.

So it is in theory. But if we have used our imagination at all vividly, as the exercise demands, the impulse of our fallen self to snap out angry words and gestures may not die as easily as has been described. It will probably go on breaking in upon our mental repetition of the Saying, dispel the feeling enshrined in it, and threaten to pass into words and actions. In other words, our fallen self will struggle for its existence like a cornered beast, even in the course of an exercise, as it certainly will much more violently in some real-life situation we are training ourselves to meet.

As usual, and particularly in real life, we are tempted to fall back on our own resources to produce results. The most naive failure is to use our own will to inhibit the angry impulse instead of using it to keep our attention fixed on the Saying. We thereby merely cover up the impulse, and prevent it being exposed to the sanctifying work of the Saying. We present a civilised facade to our opponent, not a glimpse of the Loving Good Will of I AM.

A less naive failure is to start using our will correctly, but like Peter setting out to walk on the water lose faith.[1] That is, we start by fixing our attention on the Saying, but finding ourself distracted by the angry impulse, we force ourself to act out the part of Loving

[1] Mat. 14,30.

129

Goodness of Will. Here we shall achieve even less than with a civilised facade. For since it is we who are at work and not the Saying, the counterfeit we present is bound to be recognised as spurious. We are acting the role of I AM, in fact, which is a travesty of His incarnation. In the result we shall at best appear insincere, and may well appear ludicrous.

The best hope of overcoming these and all other failures is to keep constantly before us, until it is built into our very being, what we *essentially* are as human beings. We are the differentiated aspects of The Christ Who is the objective counterpart of The Word, the ME of His I AM. We can therefore no more *do* anything, get anything truly *done*, without Him than a reflection in a mirror can move without its original.[1] Whatever we may appear to do apart from Him is mere churning of water. The deeper this essential fact is rooted in us, the easier we shall find it to recapture our grip on the Saying we are mentally repeating. The theology it represents will again inform our mind, the feeling it enshrines again fill our heart, and it will again direct our will. So the Loving Goodness of the Will of I AM must in some measure be expressed through us as the situation demands.

In so far as all this happens, the unfriendly group facing us cannot possibly remain unaffected. At least some of them are bound to regard us more kindly, however slightly. To that extent they are purged of their negative, death-bound hostility. In other words, they will be that much more truly alive. Thus, in the degree that we let the Saying work in us, and the Bread of Life is thereby given to them through us, they will receive life. The inexorable fact is that they stand to receive a measure of life or death, in this particular situation, according to our resolution to let the Saying work in us and its Spirit direct and rule what we say or do.

This review of the situation before us, imaginary but quite certain to confront us in some form or another in the course of our ministry, simply because we have charge of a parish and have to exercise authority in it, should help us to attune our will to be used by the Saying in the coming Silence. We prepare for this part of the exercise, the most important of all, as described in the previous chapter. We allow a few seconds in which to imagine the scene

---

[1] Jn. 15,5 RV

130

in our study as vividly as we can, without losing grip of the Saying. We see the unfriendly faces, hear the harsh voice of the warden, and feel the angry reaction rising in us, reinforced by apprehension. Then we confront this impulse with the Saying which we begin mentally to repeat.

"I AM the Bread of Life . . . which I will give . . . for
the life of the world".

As we repeat the Saying, we go on confronting the impulse with it, as though rubbing a stain in soap, pressing a rusty blade to the grindstone, exposing a septic sore to the disinfectant. We *grind* the impulse into the Saying. If the impulse resists dissolution, we may add another Saying to the one we are repeating. "Your ways are not MY Ways . . . I AM the Bread of Life . . . which I will give . . . for the life of the world".[1] (The original is slightly different and has been adapted to suit our context without altering its essential meaning). As the Saying begins to take possession of us and work in us, the impulse dies away. The living presence of the Saying in us begins to build up towards some appropriate action. Since the situation we are describing is trivial, the appropriate act of self-giving will be trivial too, probably no more than a word, a gesture, a mere glance signifying goodwill. We do not imagine this, as it might lead to self-dramatisation, which of course only feeds the fallen self, and might impede the "free course" of the Saying. The Saying alone can bring about the inimitable act of The SELF, on however small a scale. So we continue mentally repeating the Saying in the imagined presence of the opponent in our study, until he ceases to be our opponent and fades out of the picture in that guise, leaving us possessed by the Saying.

" I AM the Bread of Life . . . which I will give . . . for
the life of the world".

Ten to fifteen minutes' silence.

We end this last Silence of the exercise with the same simple act of thanksgiving and self-offering as was mentioned at the end of the last chapter. If this self-offering is to be serious, it must include an explicit resolution to continue the exercise every day as described at the end of that chapter. It may be convenient to sum up the points mentioned there under three heads.

[1] Isa. 55,8.

131

First, a card should be inscribed with the full Saying with the watchword at the top: "I will give". Next, time should be set aside at the very least every morning and evening, and if possible at one or two other times of the day, when we can let the Saying dwell in us for ten to fifteen minutes with the least risk of interruption. Last, the watchword at least, and if possible the whole Saying, should be recalled while falling asleep, when waking, and whenever else this can be done during the day. This is especially important, and fruitful, whenever we are mentally or physically inactive and the fallen self is liable to be more than usually obtrusive.

Chapter 8

The Embodiment of Divine Wisdom

[1]

In so far as we have received, assimilated, expressed and thereby embodied the Saying signifying the Loving Goodness of the Will of I AM, we have participated in the First Moment of His creative procession, His self-unfoldment from the hidden depth of His ineffable Unity. We are therefore as fit as we can be at this stage of our spiritual growth to try to participate in the Second Moment of His self-unfoldment. This is the Moment in which, in the Mysterious Wisdom of His Heart, He conceives the Idea of the knowable Reality fulfilled in Man.

Strictly of course we should speak of *Her* Heart, since this is the feminine, maternal aspect of I AM, but we avoid doing so in order to safeguard the indivisible triunity of the Divine Personality. As we saw before, we are obliged to consider the Will, Heart and Mind of I AM in succession, analytically, only because we ourselves are still limited by time, and are learning "by numbers" to *be* what He eternally and changelessly *is*. Since this process of learning involves the extremely subtle relationship between our fallen self and our True Self, and cannot be understood too clearly, it is worth illustrating it with another analogy.

Each one of us is learning through suffering to manifest in corporeal terms, in his own particular manner, the Truth, Beauty and Goodness which I AM universally manifests in spiritual terms. We may therefore see ourselves, not only as a distorted reflection in process of becoming a perfect image of our spiritual original, but as a glove growing increasingly pliable and obedient to the "godly motions" of the spiritual hand within us. The natural hide of each glove begins by being crude and stiff, and is broken into response

133

to the three primary "godly motions" only by degrees, one after the other.

Our first task, as usual, is to marshal our theological knowledge of the Second Moment as succinctly as possible, both in order to select from the Bible the Saying which will best signify the Moment for us at our present stage, and in order to attune our mind to receive the Saying. Since the Second Moment is intelligible only as the outcome of the First, we had better recapitulate this in a few words. In the First Moment I AM breaks and gives away His SELF for the life of all things. Since nothing conceivable can be more useful for all things, His Loving Will in making this perfect sacrifice is perfectly Good. And since nothing has life prior to His Loving Goodness of Will, it is irresistible. There is nothing to resist it. All that is effected by His Will is therefore perfectly good too.[1]

We now come to the Second Moment. Since His Will, which we have also called His originating, paternal aspect is irresistible, it takes instant effect. The next facet of His SELF to be manifested is therefore the one in which this effect fully takes place. This facet is His Heart, which we have also called His receiving, maternal aspect. Since His Will is irresistibly originating, His Heart is perfectly receptive. This receptivity is thus not passive but most vitally active. From its own standpoint, this vital receptivity is the equivalent of attraction. In that sense His Heart may be said to attract His Will, and thereby to manifest its Mystery or Beauty. In giving the fullest possible effect to the Goodness of His Will, His Heart also manifests its Wisdom. The impact of the Loving Goodness of His Will upon the Mysterious Wisdom of His Heart results in the vital feeling in which the all-inclusive Idea is conceived. It is the Divine Idea of all things whatsoever, of the knowable Reality, fulfilled in Man. Since the Idea is conceived by the impact of His Loving Goodness of Will upon the Mysterious Wisdom of His Heart, it is perfectly beautiful as well as perfectly good. So in the Second Moment of His creative procession out of His ineffable Unity, I AM in the Mysterious Wisdom of His Heart conceives the Idea of the knowable Reality, fulfilled in Man, in all its Beauty and Goodness. Let us note here again,

[1] Gen. 1, 31; Jas. 1,17.

134

especially for practical purposes, that irrefutable Wisdom issues only from Love, and Beauty only from Goodness.

This brief review of the Second Moment of the self-unfolding procession of I AM enables us to search the Bible for the Saying which expresses its significance most lucidly for us, at our present stage. We need a Saying which will as far as possible signify the Wisdom in which I AM conceives the knowable Reality, whereby, having been *given* life in the First Moment, it *receives* life. To find such a Saying is less easy than in the two previous exercises. For though the Bible often mentions the Wisdom and the Heart of I AM, it nowhere records Him as explicitly declaring that He therein conceives the Idea of all things. The Bible does however contain a passage on the subject, and when two Sayings from this are combined, we have what we are looking for. Furthermore, He uses a synonym for Wisdom in one of these Sayings which is even more revealing to us. For this synonym, in evoking our own experience, clearly points us towards both the *feeling*, and the gift of *life*, which are involved in the spiritual conception of ideas. In these two Sayings I AM declares Himself to be Understanding, and as such the Source, the Mother of Life. "I AM Understanding", He says, "whoso findeth ME findeth Life".[1]

The significance of this combined Saying for our purpose does not perhaps immediately stand out as clearly as it should, if we are properly to attune our mind to its reception. And, let us remember, unless we receive it in our mind, we cannot assimilate it in our heart, still less express it by our will. A few comments, loosely strung together, may serve to hint at its significance.

In the same passage that contains the combined Saying we have chosen, I AM also declares that those who devote themselves to Him shall inherit Substance.[2] This draws attention to the close similarity between the words Understanding and Substance. Understanding is in fact largely an English version of Substance, which is derived from Latin. For our purposes, anyway, we may take them as synonymous. Philosophically, substance is that which *underlies* all its attributes. In other words, substance is that which *understands* them all. In that sense substance may be regarded

---

[1] Prov. 8,14 & 35.
[2] Prov. 8,21.

as the source or mother of them all. In that sense they may all be said to be conceived in, and to proceed from, the substance or understanding which as their mother gives them life.

Let us now consider this maternal aspect of Understanding in terms of ideas. An idea is that which underlies all its expressions and applications in thought and action, and in that sense may also be regarded as their source or mother. Now the more universal an idea is, the more prolific, vital, life-giving it is of such expressions and applications. For instance, the more universal the knowledge of a subject is, the more prolifically and diversely it can be expressed and applied to particular circumstances. The most universal idea that it is possible to conceive is the Idea of the knowable Reality. In that sense this Idea in the Wise and Understanding Heart of I AM is the Source or Mother of all things visible and invisible.

The last comment concerns a colloquial sense of the word Understanding and its life-giving aspect. By thus evoking common experience, the significance of the Sayings we have chosen is perhaps brought home to us most vividly of all. We speak of a person being "understanding" when he is able to enter into some situation of ours so well as to see it as we do ourselves. The more he shares the ideas which govern our situation, the more "understanding" he is. His thoughts and actions are in harmony with ours because they spring from the same or kindred ideas. Therefore in the degree that he understands us in our situation, he is able to participate in it as we do. His understanding enables him to support, encourage, vitalise us as he never could without it. His lack of understanding indeed has a distinctly devitalising effect on us. In this sense I AM is the Supreme Understanding which vitalises the whole knowable Reality.

These few comments should point us towards the theological meaning of the two Sayings we have selected to signify the Second Moment of I AM's creative procession, the Second Moment of His self-unfoldment in which, in the Mysterious Wisdom of His Heart, He conceives the Idea of the whole knowable Reality. "I AM Understanding . . . whoso findeth ME findeth Life". The whole knowable Reality is fulfilled in Man, and posseses two main aspects, spiritual and corporeal. These Words are therefore uttered by the Mother of God and Man; by the Mother of God in the sense that

Spiritual Man, as the Divine Idea of Man, is the Son of God; by the Mother of Man in the sense that Corporeal Man, as the incarnation of the Divine Idea, is the objective counterpart of Spiritual Man. And because the Mysterious Wisdom of His Heart springs from the Loving Goodness of His Will, He conceives this Idea in all the Beauty of its Goodness.

The vital power of the combined Saying is greatly enhanced for us when we remember that, as corporeal human beings, we are included in this Supreme Idea. Nothing can therefore possibly destroy our *essential* beauty and goodness. If anything could, it would be greater than the Supreme Source of the knowable Reality, which is absurd. We are perfectly *understood* in all senses.

With our mind attuned to receive the Saying, we now prepare for the first Silence of the exercise. As before, we adopt the proper posture, relax bodily tensions, and sharpen our power of concentration by fixing our whole attention upon three in- and out-going breaths. In the two previous exercises we used the air entering the lungs to symbolise two aspects of the Holy Breath of I AM in relation to us. We may now let the air symbolise the all-pervading aspect of I AM. As the air we breathe in envelops the whole earth, so I AM is above all, through all, and in all.[1] As we cannot help filling our lungs with air when we breathe in, for it is all around us, so we cannot help finding I AM within our own self when we truly seek Him there. The very entry of the air into our lungs vividly symbolises His objective presence beyond the subjective summit of our self.

Having become inwardly and outwardly still, and receptive, we then allow ourselves the two minutes in which to respond to His call to come to Him. "Come unto ME, all ye that labour and are heavy laden, and I will give you Rest". We reach inwards, beyond the summit of our self, taking with us our most painful or shameful and therefore greatest burden, as a beggar might hold out his worst sore for treatment. We trace the burden to the sins that have bred it, clearly focus these as the head and front for the time being of our fallen self, and try sincerely to renounce both them and it as the cause of all suffering.

[1] Eph. 4,6.

So far we have allowed our heaviest, and therefore most obvious, burdens to guide our self-examination and the consequent purgation of our self from its fallen state. But such burdens do not necessarily stem from our greatest sins, certainly not from our subtlest. As we find relief from our most obvious burdens, we do not become sinless. Sooner or later we must learn to control our self-examination, and thus the pattern of our purgation, by deliberately searching out the less obvious burdens that lie hidden in us, so that we may acknowledge and renounce the more subtle sins that breed them. We can do this by using whatever Saying we may be trying to receive, and the Divine Perfection it signifies, to point us to the opposite in ourselves. In the present case, for instance, we can search out, face up to, and accept a burden which is bred by our lack of Divine Wisdom in facing some problem in our life, and thereby become fully awake to the sin involved.

As soon as we become sensitive to such a lack in us, we quickly learn to recognise the burdens it breeds. If we have dealt with people by worldly wisdom not Divine Wisdom, for instance by diplomatic cunning not understanding, we may well be entangled in a web of intrigue and all its consequent troubles. To free ourselves from the web by the same methods is as problematic as finding the way out of a maze, or curing symptoms without considering their causes. No wonder S. Paul calls the wisdom of this world foolishness before Divine Wisdom.[1] Such a sin, really a form of faithlessness, is obviously more subtle than, say, some sin of commission.[2] Thus it may at first take longer to expose and renounce than the two minutes we allow for self-examination. In that case, as already mentioned, the connection between any particular burden and sin of that kind may have to be clarified at some other time.

Let us suppose, however, that our self-knowledge enables us to grasp the connection during the two minutes' period, and thereby to pin-point this subtler feature of our fallen self. We renounce the foolishness of worldly wisdom and its source, our fallen self. We drive this home by recalling, as in the previous exercise, that in renouncing our fallen self we are doing the best we can to liberate our True Self from its tomb. In this light some Words of I AM

[1] 1 Cor. 1,20.
[2] Rom. 14,23.

assume a meaning for us which they certainly did not convey before we were spiritually awake. "Behold", He says, "thy days approach that thou must die".[1] We recognise these Words, so ominous to the fallen self, as a promise of our coming freedom. For the fallen self alone is mortal.

The Saying we are preparing to receive signifies the living, vital aspect of I AM. It may complete our preparation for the Silence if we follow up the promise of our coming liberation with some other Words in which I AM affirms His supremely vital aspect. "I AM alive for evermore", He declares.[2] If we put these two Sayings together, they bring out most vividly the abysmal contrast between the fallen self we seek to "put off" and the Supreme SELF we seek to "put on".[3] "Thou must die . . . I AM alive for evermore".

We now silence all our own thoughts, however exalted, and fill our mind with nothing but the Saying we have chosen to signify the Second Moment of the creative self-unfoldment of I AM, repeating this mentally just fast enough to exclude all else.

"I AM Understanding . . . whoso findeth ME findeth Life".

Ten to fifteen minutes' silence.

[2]

The Silence over, we prepare for the next one by attuning our heart to assimilate the feeling with which the Saying is charged, that is to say, the Feeling of Life-giving Wisdom. We do so as before by choosing some priestly act to point us towards this inexpressible feeling. Theologically, the administration of the Wine in the Holy Eucharist is as significant of this as that of the Bread in the previous chapter. For the Wine signifies the Blood of Christ, which in turn signifies the Life of I AM, as the Bread and the Body signify His Being. But the experience of giving the Wine differs so little from that of giving the Bread that we must look for another. The act which suits our purpose well is the one of hearing a confession and giving the penitent absolution.

The first feature we should consider in the adminstration of this Sacrament is the priest's attitude towards the penitent from the

[1] Deut. 31,14.
[2] Rev. 1,18.
[3] Eph. 4,22-24; Rom. 13,14.

moment he sees him. Knowing the penitent's need and the ability the priest has been given to satisfy it, his whole attitude towards the sufferer is one of goodwill. This Sacrament, like any other, is essentially a means of vitalising mankind in the struggle to fulfil the purpose of its existence. The priest therefore seeks to administer the Sacrament in the manner best suited to relieve the penitent of the debilitating unhappiness he has brought upon himself by his sins, to counsel him in his efforts to destroy his fallen self which breeds his sins and therefore his suffering, and finally to invigorate him in his struggle to awaken to his True Self. No matter what the priest may actually say, he achieves these objects only in the degree that he is *certain* of the penitent's essential goodness as a human being. However great the penitent's sins may be, his True Self is alive in him. Otherwise he would not be a fallen self, or a human being, or indeed have any existence at all. For I AM, of Whom his True Self is a differentiation, is the Source, Ground and Goal of all things. And the priest's certitude is complete when it is based, not only on theology, but on his own experience.

This attitude towards the penitent from the start, prior to any knowledge of him as a person, enables the priest to taste something of the unconditioned Loving Goodness of the Will of I AM, Who loves before there is yet anything to love. So he is enabled to taste something of the Wisdom and Understanding in which I AM conceives the penitent, and all other things, in his essential beauty and goodness. For Wisdom is the outcome of Love.

The next feature we touch on is the priest's attitude while hearing the confession. As the penitent tells his sins, the priest's goodwill towards him does not flag; on the contrary, it is reinforced by compassion. His vocation keeps him from illusions regarding the nature and consequences of sin. His own experience teaches him that the greater a man's sins, the greater must be his present and future suffering. Of all men, the priest must appreciate the inexorable fact that a man reaps as he sows.[1] His personal experience teaches him that the more clearly a man sees this *fatal* or *karmic* link between his sins and his sufferings, the more determined he grows to destroy their cause, his fallen self. Therefore he does not slur over the penitent's sins and sufferings, but encourages him to uncover them

[1] Gal. 6,7.

fully, as a doctor would a patient's symptons. By this "clinical" attitude the priest affirms, and helps the penitent to accept, the fact that no sin can possibly destroy the essential perfection in which I AM in His Wisdom and Understanding conceives him, and all other things. Otherwise he could undo by his sins what I AM does, which is as impossible as it would be for an image in a mirror to wipe out its original. At the same time the priest helps the penitent to see his sins and sufferings as a spur to awaken to his essential perfection, in order to possess it consciously as his own.

This attitude of the priest towards the penitent enables him to begin tasting something of Divine Wisdom. Although I AM conceives man as perfect, his least imperfection cannot be hidden from His Understanding. Yet I AM in His Wisdom at the same time foreknows the perfection that man unfolds with increasing awareness as a result of his suffering.

The next feature we may note is the priest's attitude in giving the penitent counsel and penance. Here his attitude is as "understanding" as possible in the colloquial sense. This enables him to give such counsel and penance as will help the penitent, having clearly accepted the link between his suffering and his fallen self, to destroy the cause of that suffering. There is, of course, no trace of condemnation in his attitude towards the penitent.

So he is enabled to taste something of the complete absence of judgment in Divine Wisdom.[1] Justice itself, let alone mercy, forbids judgment. For without man's fall into sin and his consequent suffering, he could no more fulfil the purpose of his creation, could no more learn to express the Glory of God in corporeal terms, than a creative worker can become a master craftsman without "sweating blood", to use a current phrase which is more significant than most of those who use it probably realise.[2] In His Wisdom and Understanding I AM never changes in His conception of man as perfect, no matter how far he falls from that state. His fall is never more than extrinsic, accidental in the philosophical sense, and can never affect his essential perfection.

The last feature we need touch on is the priest's attitude in giving the penitent absolution from his sins. His whole manner

---

[1] Jn. 3,17; Jn. 12,47.
[2] Gen. 3,19; Lk. 22,44.

141

in doing this seeks to convince the penitent as deeply as possible that his sins are wholly wiped out.[1] He will have to suffer their consequences.[2] But if the priest's counsel has been worth anything, he will understand and accept this correction.[3] It is the process of his purgation and his instruction, whereby he learns to manifest the Glory of God in corporeal terms.[4] There can be no possible doubt of his being wholly cleansed of his past sins. For in the last analysis, I AM blots out man's sins because not to do so would be to cut man off from manifesting the Glory of God. Not to blot them out would nullify His own self-revelation, self-expression, self-unfoldment. Hence He declares the ultimate reason for His cancellation of human sin. "I, even I, AM He that blotteth out thy transgressions for MINE Own sake, and will not remember thy sins".[5] As the penitent goes out into workaday life, the priest cannot help sharing in the vitalising joy and courage with which he faces whatever further trials, temptations, falls, sufferings lie ahead of him.

So the priest is enabled to taste something of the *vitalising* certainty of Divine Wisdom and Understanding, which cannot possibly be deflected from conceiving all things in their essential beauty and goodness. The experience of being the channel of giving this certainty to another human being is perhaps the most vivid taste a man can have of the dynamic, life-giving, inspiring quality of Divine Wisdom and Understanding. In the light of this experience it is impossible to doubt that anything can mar the immaculate perfection of the whole knowable Reality eternally pouring forth from the Spiritual Womb of I AM. This feeling of certainty is the very hall-mark of His all-foreseeing, all-forgiving, all-foreordaining Wisdom and Understanding.

These reflections on the administration of the Sacrament of Penance may help us to attune our heart to the inexpressible Divine Feeling enshrined in the Saying. We now resolutely put away all memories evoked by these reflections, and concentrate our whole attention on the mental repetition of the Saying, seeking to draw from it the

---

[1] Isa. 1,18.
[2] Mat. 5,26.
[3] Jer. 2,19.
[4] Heb. 12,5-10.
[5] Isa. 43,25.

Divine Feeling with which it is charged.

"I AM Understanding . . . whoso findeth ME findeth Life".

Ten to fifteen minutes' silence.

[3]

After doing our best to taste the feeling with which the Saying is charged, we are as fit as we can be for the last Silence in which we shall train our will to let the Saying work in us. "MY servant shall deal wisely", declares I AM.[1] It is impossible to deal wisely in the full sense without His Wisdom, without being inspired by His Holy Spirit of Wisdom and Understanding, as uttered by the Saying.

We begin our preparation for the last Silence of this exercise as before, by choosing a watchword to represent the whole Saying. Its essence is dynamic, vitalising, life-giving Understanding. Let the watchword be: "I AM Understanding". Having chosen it, we straightaway make an act of will to use it in place of our own will in trying to "deal wisely" in the situation we are about to imagine. So, by getting a grip of the Sword of the Spirit, we do our best to surrender to the guidance of the Holy Spirit within us. Thus armed, we are ready to imagine the situation and thereby to attune our will to the surrender we shall practise in the coming Silence.

As already mentioned, the situation is a continuation of our ordeal with the dominating warden. If we are to act with life-giving Wisdom, it is clearly not enough merely to reject his proposal for "popularising" the Liturgy, however kindly. We shall have to convince him that to omit the Epistle is not the way to this. Otherwise he will be left frustrated rather than vitalised. Let us begin by sketching the situation as it has developed out of our last meeting with him, backed by his supporters. The relationship between him and ourselves has of course again altered.

Let us suppose that because we were able to surrender to the Holy Spirit of Love sufficiently to meet his attempt at coercion with kindness, and not with the anger characteristic of our fallen self, he

---

[1] Isa. 52,13 RV.

143

has lost the united backing of his supporters. This is inevitable, for in the degree that I AM has been "lifted up" in us, He has "drawn them" to Himself in us.[1] Some have become neutral in the dispute, some almost friendly to us. The effect on our opponent is to make him so afraid of not getting his way as to become bitterly hostile. As a result he invents some malicious slander about us. Being a worthy opponent and no fool, he chooses some story which is both plausible and well fitted to discredit our spiritual authority as parish priest. He collects the remainder of his supporters, all hostile too, and demands another interview with us.

We can increase our knowledge of our fallen self, and the effectiveness of the exercise, by imagining the slander in detail. For if it is plausible, it must contain some grain of truth, due to some weakness of ours.

We imagine ourselves back in our study, facing the shrunken but far more hostile group. They know that we know of the slander circulating about us, and the atmosphere is explosive. Their leader the warden brusquely repeats his demand for "a more popular" Liturgy. Either his demand is accepted, he implies, or he and his supporters will start a campaign to eject us. Although they cannot eject us, we know that they can so hinder our work that we may prefer to go ourselves. At that moment we see little in the group, and especially their leader, that is not distinctly ugly and evil. We feel that their interference in the parish priest's inalienable sphere has passed the tolerable limit. To treat them with kindness and gentleness no longer seems justifiable. As we glance from one scowling face to another, alarm rises in us. As we remember the slander for which the group is responsible, alarm is reinforced with indignation. As we consider their wish to mangle the Liturgy, indignation is reinforced with the kind of fury which underlies religious wars. We feel the impulse rising in us to silence the leader of the group at all costs, by interrupting him, banging the table, throwing him out of the door.

This is the point, before our fallen self explodes in words or actions of condemnation which will damage our work quite as much as the group can, at which to recall the watchword. "I AM Understanding". As we saw in the previous chapter, this may not be

[1] Jn. 12,32.

144

easy even in an imaginary situation. Let us suppose, however, that our will has benefitted by our training since then and enables us quickly to concentrate our attention on the watchword. With our attention thus distracted from the incipient reaction of our fallen self, we are able to recall the whole Saying. "I AM Understanding . . . whoso findeth ME findeth Life".

It may be unflattering to remember that small children are similarly distracted from misbehaving. If so, we are reminded how far we still are from spiritually full-grown manhood.

As we mentally repeat the Saying in the face of the impulse of our fallen self, something of its general theological significance is probably the first to come home to us. In signifying the Second Moment of the creative self-unfoldment of I AM, we are reminded that it is the outcome of the First Moment. It is only because I AM in the Loving Goodness of His Will breaks and gives away His SELF for the life of the world, that in the Wisdom of His Heart He conceives the Idea of the Reality in all its beauty and goodness. In His Wisdom He therefore perfectly understands the purpose of man's fall from his essentially inviolable perfection. His Understanding invigorates, vitalises, inspires man's struggle to profit by his fall in order to attain the purpose of his creation. Thus in His Wisdom He foreknows man as having attained his destiny, perfect in all the beauty of his goodness.

As something of the theological significance of the Saying comes home to us, we should be reminded of the Divine Feeling it is charged with. We may remember this in the abstract, however, and find it impossible genuinely to feel any Wisdom and Understanding in the teeth of the reaction of our fallen self. We can only cling to the mental repetition of the Saying. If the Feeling enshrined in the Saying remains an abstraction, we may have to re-experience something of Divine Love from which Wisdom derives, by recalling the Saying we used in the previous exercise. We may even have to re-experience something of Holiness of which Divine Love is the first manifestation, before trying again to feel Divine Wisdom. This may involve recalling the priestly act of giving the Blessing, the Eucharistic Bread and the Absolution. It is as though we reinforced our attempt to feel Divine Wisdom with all our previous experience of I AM as He comes forth from the unknowable depth of His Unity.

Let us suppose that we are at last enabled genuinely to feel something of Divine Wisdom and Understanding. We try to see the hostile group facing us, and particularly its leader the warden, in this light. As we continue mentally repeating the Saying, as though it were addressed to our opponent who has now declared himself our enemy, the feeling begins to replace the fear, indignation, even fury which threatens to explode in words and actions directed at him. We begin to recognise that the good intention to attract people to the Holy Eucharist is among his motives. This does not blind us to his malice. If it did, we would be fools not wise. But because the Saying is beginning to possess us, and its Spirit to guide us, we understand the good intention which has misfired in malice. The more we understand this, the more superficial the *blot* on his good intention appears, and the more insistently his good intention calls for redirection, encouragement, fulfilment.

As we thus let the Saying work in us, we become able to "deal wisely" with our enemy and to guide his intention to its fulfilment. In so doing we cease to see him as our enemy, and free him from seeing us as his enemy. So we overcome and destroy this particular manifestation of enmity, and in that sense destroy the enemy. We may as usual be tempted to imagine what words or gestures to use in "dealing wisely" with the warden. To do so would be to use our own will in order to act out the part of Divine Wisdom. It is impossible to realise too clearly that the proper use of the will is to give "free course" to the Saying to work itself out in us. Led by the Holy Spirit of the Saying, it will be "given us" exactly what to say and do.[1] The more we are led by the Holy Spirit, the less we shall probably be "given" to say or do.

So it is in theory, as we saw in the previous exercise, before we went on to suggest a few ways of overcoming the commonest failures to put theory into practice. It would be tedious to go over the same ground again here. If what was said then has been forgotten, the relevant pages should be re-read.[2]

The situation we have just imagined has helped us to attune our will to its proper work in that situation, which is to hold our attention firmly on the mental repetition of the Saying, and let it work itself

---

[1] Mat. 10,19 & 20.
[2] Pages 129 etc.

out in us. So we are ready for the last Silence, in which we shall exercise our will in actually doing this, in the imagination. As in the previous exercise, we allow a few seconds to imagine ourselves back in our study, facing the hostile group led by the warden. We imagine his facial expression, his words, his gestures in all the offensive hostility we have described. Then we allow the reaction of our fallen self to boil up to the highest degree of intensity short of discharging itself and distracting us from the exercise. The more vividly we use our imagination, the more effectively the exercise will work for the embodiment of the Saying in us. And to that extent for the incarnation of I AM in us.

With our eyes fixed on our enemy, if possible meeting his eyes, as our fallen self is about to erupt, we recall the watchword. "I AM Understanding". We mentally repeat this until we can fix our attention on the whole Saying. "I AM Understanding . . . whoso findeth ME findeth Life". Our eyes continue to meet our enemy's, but our attention is fixed on the Saying. At each mental repetition we confront the emotions of our fallen self with the Saying, as though exposing useless rubbish to the fire. Natural resources are indeed useless, and worse, as soon as we begin the effort to live supernaturally. As the Saying starts to possess us, the Spirit of Life-giving Wisdom and Understanding pouring forth from I AM begins to flow through us upon our enemy. He ceases to be our enemy. We become aware of him only as the recipient, together with ourselves and all other things invisible and visible, of the boundless Grace pouring forth from I AM. It is "given us" what to say or do, and we do it spontaneously; yet not we, but I AM in us.[1]

"I AM Understanding . . . whoso findeth ME findeth Life".

Ten to fifteen minutes' silence.

The last Silence of the exercise should end, as always, with the simple thanksgiving and self-oblation mentioned at the end of the previous exercises. It is necessary to emphasise that the self-oblation should include a resolution to use the watchword and Saying every day. For without this what we offer to I AM is greater rubbish than it need be.

[1] Gal. 2,20.

147

Chapter 9

The Embodiment of Divine Power

[1]

In so far as we have embodied the Saying signifying the Wisdom of I AM, and thus participated in the Second Moment of His creative self-unfoldment, we are as fit as we can be at this stage to participate in the Third Moment. Here His self-unfoldment into spiritual manifestation is fulfilled and His Power is revealed. This is the Moment in which He all-powerfully *does* all things. Since we can *do* nothing without Him in the full sense of getting anything *done,* this Moment is of particular practical importance for us. For this reason alone we must marshal our knowledge of what He does in this Moment particularly clearly and succinctly. This will at the same time help us to search the Bible all the more intelligently for the Saying which signifies what He does, in the vivid manner which is most suited for such practical use.

Since His Power issues from His Wisdom, and this from His Love, we had better start at the point where He begins His self-unfoldment from His ineffable Unity. He begins it where, in the Loving Goodness of His Will, He *breaks* and *gives away* His SELF, thus establishing the Goodness of the whole knowable Reality whose manifestation begins at this point. Thereupon, in the Mysterious Wisdom of His Heart, He *conceives* the Idea of the knowable Reality, fulfilled in Man, in all the Beauty of its Goodness. Finally, by the Power of His True Knowing, His All-conscious Mind, He *expresses* the Idea of the knowable Reality, fulfilled in Man, in all its Truth and Beauty and Goodness.

This intellectual expression of the all-inclusive Idea necessarily involves the two complementary aspects of inner and outer, subjective and objective, spiritual and corporeal. Therefore, I AM first expresses the inner, subjective, spiritual aspect of the knowable Reality by *being* it, by *constituting* it in all its Truth, Beauty and Goodness.

148

He then immediately expresses the outer, objective, corporeal aspect of the knowable Reality by *knowing*, and thus *creating*, it in all its Truth, Beauty and Goodness. What He *knows* is thus the corporeal counterpart of what He *is* spiritually. In other words, these two aspects of the knowable Reality are the ME and the I respectively of His indivisible all-inclusive I AM.

Having thus expressed the Idea of the knowable Reality subjectively and objectively in all its Truth, Beauty and Goodness, He *upholds* both these aspects by the same means. That is to say, by His Love, Wisdom and Power He unceasingly constitutes and knows the two aspects respectively in all their Truth, Beauty and Goodness. And apart from this the knowable Reality could not *be*.

Finally, by His Love, Wisdom and Power He draws into His SELF the knowable Reality fulfilled in Man in its *corporeal* aspect. He does this through its highest element, Corporeal Man, by drawing human Selves into union with His SELF. So by His presence in the endless multitude and diversity of human Selves, aware of His SELF as their True Self, He constitutes the *corporeal* aspect of the Reality.

So by His Love, Wisdom and Power He fills Heaven and Earth, the spiritual and corporeal aspects of the Reality, with Truth, Beauty and Goodness. He thereby fulfils His self-unfoldment and manifests the Glory of the Holy One. He fills Heaven with Truth, Beauty and Goodness — by His SELF. He fills Earth with Truth, Beauty and Goodness — by the sanctified Selves of His saints. Since Earth is the sphere in which we are still learning to be saints, which from His all-inclusive standpoint is already accomplished, we must particularly clearly recall the threefold manner in which He fills Earth — by us — with Truth, Beauty and Goodness. This threefold manner is due to the complexity of the corporeal Reality, the realm of multiplicity, diversity and change. The first manner is as the single primal triunity, the corporeal counterpart of His spiritual SELF called The Christ, at the summit of corporeal manifestation beyond space, time and change. The second is as His SELF differentiated into the endless multitude and diversity of Selves extending throughout space, time and change. The third is as His SELF holding all Selves together in a single Body both in and beyond all space, time and change. Inwardly all are one with Him and each

149

other; outwardly all are separate and uniquely distinct. So the corporeal Reality fulfilled in Man, down to its outermost conditions of space, time and change, exactly corresponds with the spiritual as its objective counterpart. And so the I and the ME of I AM fills Heaven and Earth with Truth, Beauty and Goodness and thereby manifests the Glory of the Holy One beyond all.

This recapitulation of the Third Moment, wherein I AM does all things whatsoever, helps us to search the Bible for the Saying which will most vividly signify this for us at our present stage. Here we find a great wealth from which to choose, including some already quoted. For instance, He declares His activity to be supremely intellectual. "As I have thought, so shall it come to pass".[1] He declares His Intellect to be supremely active. "Things . . . went forth out of MY Mouth, and I showed them".[2] He declares His intellectual activity to be both subjective and objective. "The Earth, and . . . the Heavens: when I call unto them, they stand up together".[3] When He speaks of filling Heaven and Earth, we may therefore understand this not only in the static sense that He is their fulness, but in the dynamic sense of filling them up, and in the ideal sense of fulfilling them. He speaks as the Source, Ground and Goal of all things. But the Bible nowhere records him as explicitly signifying in a single Saying everything that HE *does* in creating, upholding and fulfilling all things. We therefore choose one, already quoted, in which He clearly implies this. "I AM . . . the Beginning and the Ending . . . the Almighty".[4] A few comments may remind us of the *dynamic* implications of the Saying, which particularly concern us here, and help us to attune our mind to it.

The first concerns I AM as the Beginning. As we have seen, He describes Himself in these words as the Source of all things. Let us emphasise His intellectual aspect as the Source. Things *are* simply and solely because I AM knows them, including ourselves. This being so, their whole existence from moment to moment hangs entirely upon His continued knowledge of them. He is therefore

---

[1] Isa. 14,24.
[2] Isa. 48,3.
[3] Isa. 48,13.
[4] Rev. 1,8.

the intellectual Ground or Rock upon which all things rest, as well as their intellectual Source.[1]

The next comment concerns Him as the Ending. Since nothing exists prior to or apart from His knowledge of it, His knowledge of things cannot grow. He must know all things perfectly in their essential perfection from the beginning. In their essential perfection all Selves are the differentiated aspects of His SELF. This perfection must include the inherent capacity to know all things as He knows them. When all Selves awaken to what they *essentially* are, and know even as they are known, they are fulfilled in Him.[2] From His standpoint He, Who is their Fulfilment, is fulfilled in them. Therefore, when He declares Himself to be the Ending, He signifies Himself to be the Fulfilment in this dual sense, the Consummation of all things.

The last comment concerns Him as the Almighty. Since all things are created, upheld and fulfilled solely by being known by Him, every conceivable event must in *some* sense be an expression of His intellectual activity. He therefore declares Himself to be the Almightly in the fullest and most exact sense. If He stopped knowing things, they would instantly vanish as though they had never been. His Power is absolute in the fullest sense. Hence He explicitly declares, when incarnate, that all Power is given to Him in Heaven and in Earth.[3] So also S. Paul declares that "there is no Power but of God".[4] We must therefore accept the fact that even such power as evil possesses must ultimately derive from His Omnipotence.

This deduction, which is obviously of great practical importance, may at first seem questionable. If so, let us remember that its truth is confirmed by I AM Himself. When He stands before Pilate, incarnate in Jesus, He refuses to plead for His life. Pilate tells Him that he has power of life and death over Him. "Thou couldest have no power at all against ME", He replies, "except it were given thee from above".[5] Pilate then proceeds to use the power given to him. We regard the destruction of a worthless man who is innocent of crime as evil. The physical destruction of the perfect

[1] 1 Cor. 10,4.
[2] 1 Cor. 13,12.
[3] Mat. 28,18.
[4] Rom. 13,1.
[5] Jn. 19,11.

man who is innocent must therefore be as evil an act as is conceivable. Yet the power to carry it out came from I AM, as He Himself incarnate explicitly declares. The power came from I AM, of course, so that its evil use might produce incomparably greater good. In the light of that good, the evil is seen to be necessary. Hence I AM declares that He creates evil.[1]

This may appear startling, for we are still far from having overcome the evil which stands in the way of goodness in our lives. The opposition between good and evil is very real for fallen selves struggling to attain goodness; evil, ugliness and falsity have to be fought to overcoming point. But beyond the relatively small area of the corporeal Reality affected by the struggle evil has no raison d'être and therefore no existence. This knowledge is an added stimulus to seek Power from I AM in order to overcome evil wherever it does exist. We are in practical touch here with what we have already considered in theory, when it is a good deal more easy to accept the part played by evil in the attainment of goodness, by ugliness in the attainment of beauty, and by falsity in the attainment of truth. Hence the suffering which is indispensable from the joy of this, for man, supremely creative work.

These comments on the Saying we have chosen should bring home to us once more the fact that we literally can *do* nothing, in the sense of getting anything *done*, without I AM.[2] All activity without Him is literally without power, rather as a machine disconnected from its engine cannot achieve, accomplish, get anything *done*. Whatever activity is without Him is random and ultimately negative, and thus sooner or later begins to undo whatever has been done by His Power. When nothing is left to undo, the machine is plainly seen to have run down. In view of the great practical importance to ourselves of the Power of I AM, we will end our preparation for the first Silence by once more tracing the derivation of His Omnipotence. He possesses absolute Power over the knowable Reality which He constitutes and knows *because* He conceives the Idea of it in His Wisdom. And He does this *because* in His Love He breaks and gives away His SELF for the sake of making His Reality knowable, that is to say, for the sake of manifesting it. Hence

---

[1] Isa. 45, 7; Amos 3,6.
[2] Jn. 15,5.

a man can have power to get anything *done* in the full sense only in so far as it is born of wisdom, and this is in turn born of sacrificial love.

With our mind attuned to receive the Saying, we are now ready for the first Silence. We adopt the proper bodily posture, relax, and concentrate attention on three in- and out-going breaths. These can be made to symbolise the Spirit of I AM in us in yet another way, and especially now the Spirit of Power. Let us hold our breath until we can no longer endure the pressure on our lungs, without losing our hold on life. We can let this pressure symbolise the irresistible Power of I AM within us, Who declares Himself to be The Life, The Living One.[1]

Having attained some measure of concentration, we recall His Comfortable Words, and allow ourselves two minutes to respond to them. "Come unto ME, all ye that labour and are heavy laden, and I will give you Rest". We are reminded that we must seek *rest* in Him before we can use His Power, as a machine must *remain* geared to its engine before it can achieve anything. Whatever our burdens may be, it must now be quite plain that they all are bred by the sin of faithlessness, in the sense of trying to do things without I AM. This state of faithlessness pin-points our fallen self more acutely than any particular sin. For in trying to do things without I AM, the fallen self proclaims its separation from I AM. This is the essence of sin, which from the standpoint of I AM may be called uselessness. So a branch is essentially useless when separate from the vine, or a mirror when cut off from light; it serves no purpose.[2]

As we progress in our exercises, these facts should become increasingly self-evident. So we are correspondingly able whole-heartedly, with our whole heart, and therefore quickly, to link our burdens with our sins, renounce them, and turn away from the fallen self that is their root. There is no better way of making this act of self-denial, in the full sense, than by recalling a Saying that once seemed ominous. "Thou must die". Without pondering it, we immediately use it to point us to the indwelling presence of Him Who utters this Saying, as He does the following. "I AM alive

[1] Jn. 14,6; Rev. 1,18 RV.
[2] Jn. 15,4; Jn. 1,9.

153

for evermore". In this way we can in a second transfer our attention from our fallen, and therefore mortal, self to the eternally Living SELF with Whom we seek to be one. Then we put away all thoughts, and allow nothing to occupy our mind but the Saying we have chosen to signify the absolute Power by which I AM *is* and *does* all things.

" I AM . . . the Beginning and the Ending . . . the Almighty".
Ten to fifteen minutes' silence.

[2]

We next turn to attune our heart to assimilate the Feeling of absolute Power with which the Saying is charged. We shall do so again by using some priestly act to point us towards the ineffable Feeling which the Saying alone can convey to us. Such a preparation is at least as necessary here as in previous exercises, because the feeling commonly suggested by the word *power* is an even greater travesty of the spiritual truth than in the case of love and wisdom. Hence what passes for power among human beings is said to corrupt, and absolute power to corrupt absolutely. For this reason alone such power is not absolute in the full sense, nor indeed power at all.

If we begin by clearly recognising this, we shall better appreciate the significance of the priestly act which points us towards the absolute Power of I AM. It is plain that if what is commonly called power tends to corrupt those who exercise it, they sooner or later become incapable of doing so. And if those over whom it is exercised become corrupted by their subjection to it, they never acquire it at all. But if they do not become corrupted, they sooner or later build up a resistance to such power, until they overthrow it. Such an uncertain, fluctuating factor in human relationships is better called *force* in order to distinguish it from the changeless, absolute Power of I AM. Ultimately force is self-destructive, which is its greatest distinction from the eternal Power of I AM by which all things are created, upheld and fulfilled.

No priestly act serves better to point us towards the ineffable Feeling of absolute Power than that of baptising a baby in arms. As the priest holds the baby over the font, its whole situation in his arms speaks, not only of his complete power over it, but of the love and wisdom from which true power is derived. Let us consider some of the features of the Rite which bring out this derivation of true power and point to its creating, upholding and fulfilling work. During those moments the priest's arms signify the "eternal dwelling place of God" for the baby. "Underneath are the everlasting arms".[1]

We begin by recalling that no fee is charged for carrying out baptisms. This may be taken to signify that the act the priest performs, whereby the child is sacramentally incorporated in The SELF and His Body the Church, is a free gift. It is in that sense an act of disinterested goodwill, and symbolises the Loving Goodness of the Will of I AM. Then follows the act of incorporation itself. The baby sacramentally receives the Holy Spirit proceeding from I AM, and since this includes the Spirit of Love, Wisdom and Power, the child's self is thereby drawn into His SELF. As we have seen, this procession of the Holy Spirit begins in the First Moment in which I AM breaks and gives away His SELF. As the priest pours the consecrated water over the baby's forehead, he thus enacts the Loving Goodness of the Will in which I AM eternally breaks and gives away His SELF for the sake of all things.

The next feature we consider is the baby's reception into "the congregation of Christ's flock" immediately after being baptised. As the priest holds the baby in his arms, the innocence of this newly-enlisted "soldier and servant" of Christ is plain. Equally plainly that innocence will be lost, which will be paid for in suffering. This must be so before the innocence can be won back in order to be possessed as holiness. There is no doubt of that holiness. For the baby is signed with the sign of the cross, and has thereby not only entered upon the path of suffering which leads to holiness, but has received thereby the affirmation of its own essential holiness. As the priest looks down on the face of the newly enlisted soldier and servant, who at that moment is probably bawling his head off as though aware of being launched upon the long and painful way to holiness, no human being is easier to regard with compassionate understanding. The priest sees that human being's pristine innocence, fall, and ultimate holiness spread out before him simultaneously. So

---

[1] Deut. 33,27 RV.

in the act of signing the baby with the sign of the cross, the priest sees it with something of the Wisdom and Understanding of I AM.

The last feature we must consider is the baby's relationship with the priest during the Rite. In this context, the baby's whole welfare depends upon the priest, both spiritually and corporeally. His power over the baby in these moments is as complete as is possible in any human relationship. The baby owes its incipient spiritual life on this earth, in its Catholic Christian form, to his act of baptising it. Without Baptism, it will not grow spiritually in that form. And the baby owes its incipient corporeal existence on this earth, in its healthy form, to his holding it firmly in his arms. If he lets go of it, it may never grow physically healthy. His complete power over the baby ensures that he uses it wholly for the baby's welfare. He is not to be deflected by the baby's acceptance or rejection of what he does for it. This experience of the priest, as he stands at the font with the baby in his arms, thus most truly and objectively points him towards the ineffable Feeling of absolute Power in which I AM creates, upholds and fulfills all things whatsoever.

Having with these reflections attuned our heart to assimilate the ineffable Divine Feeling, we dismiss all the thoughts and experiences called up thereby, and once more begin mentally to repeat the Saying. It alone can communicate to us the Feeling of Omnipotence with which it is charged. For the Saying *is* the very Spirit of Power by which I AM constitutes the Reality in its spiritual aspect and creates its corporeal counterpart; the Power by which He indraws, fulfills and thus constitutes the Reality in its corporeal aspect. This Omnipotence is the root of all activity which accomplishes, achieves, *does* anything whatsover.

"I AM . . . the Beginning and the Ending . . . the Almighty".
Ten to fifteen minutes' silence.

[3]

We now prepare for the last Silence of this exercise in which we shall train our will to let the Saying actually work in us. The situation we shall imagine will be our encounter with the church-warden, and it will be the finally decisive encounter. In the degree that we can surrender to the Saying, we shall become a channel of the Love, Wisdom and Power in which I AM *does* all things whatsoever. That degree will be the exact measure of true power we shall dispose of in our coming spiritual trial of strength with our opponent, now our declared enemy. It should be plain to us by now that the trial of strength will essentially be between our awakening True Self and our fallen self. The warden thus merely represents the objective counterpart of "our adversary the devil" within our own selves.

The more vividly we can imagine what follows, the more useful the exercise will be. (Although it would obviously be out of place to set out here a dramatically graphic scene such as might be in place in fiction). We begin our preparation, as always, by choosing a watchword which will represent the whole Saying. Since this is the last exercise to be set out in detail, we shall imagine ourselves to be tried as severely as is likely in the relatively trivial situation we have chosen. It is therefore all the more necessary for us not only to have a well-chosen watchword but to be familiar with it. The best of weapons loses much of its effectiveness by unfamiliarity. Let it be: "I AM . . . the Almighty". We straightaway repeat it a few times and make an act of will to use it in our final trial. On the last occasion we recognised that to "deal wisely" with our enemy we had to convince him that his proposal for a "popular" Liturgy would defeat its own purpose. If we are to deal with him by the Power of I AM in our coming interview, we shall have to persuade him not merely to abandon his view, but willingly to accept and support ours.[1]

We begin by imagining the situation as it has developed out of the meeting described in the previous exercise. Let us suppose that on that occasion we surrendered to the Saying so as to "deal wisely" enough with the group of our opponents as to convince them of the impossibility of their proposal. As often happens, this was probably due less to the impact of reason on their minds than of goodwill and understanding on their hearts in the face of their threats. The warden alone, whom we must imagine to be a tough opponent to the end, has reverted to his original position, and is now more determined than ever to get his way. Alarmed at finding himself isolated, infuriated by unaccustomed opposition, he is now our

[1] 1 Cor. 2,4.

157

bitterest enemy. He demands to see us for a final interview which he intends to be decisive.

As the time for the imagined encounter approaches, we unite ourselves as best we can with the Source of Power by recalling the watchword, not only more frequently than in a less trying situation, but more vitally. For instance, instead of merely letting it pass through the mind, as we do when it will not be immediately needed, we also try to taste something of the Feeling it enshrines. Since the Omnipotence of I AM implies His Wisdom which implies His Love, we thereby realise His whole indwelling presence as vividly as such brief recollection allows. In the degree that we thus abide in Him, we know Him abiding in us.[1] This intensified recollection of the watchword, and the heightened awareness of the indwelling presence of I AM that results, may be illustrated by focussing the eye on a light, so that what has hitherto been seen as a diffused glow becomes a sharply defined and much more intense point. During such moments The SELF extinguishes our fallen self, as intense light kills all lesser light, and we are in some degree one with Him.

It may be thought that the following scene is too exaggerated in the context of the trivial situation we have chosen for our exercises. But it is not far removed from fact, and in any case as in war it is wise to train for difficult rather than easy conditions. At last the crucial encounter is at hand. As we imagine the familiar footsteps at our study door, we take a grip as it were of the watchword. The enemy enters our study. Without bothering to disguise his bitter hostility, he abruptly demands if we intend carrying out his proposal to "popularise" the Liturgy. We reject the proposal. Let us imagine what follows as vividly as we can. Our enemy loses his temper. We see his scowling stare fixed on us, watch him raise his arm and feel a stinging blow on our face. Then we feel the reaction of our fallen self surging up in us. It is, let us say, a furious impulse to put our fist through his face.

As this is the last exercise to be set out in detail, let us note this critical point with particular care. This will help us to design and practise other exercises on the same principles to suit our particular needs, that is to say, the strongest features of our fallen self. This critical point is the moment between some natural stimulus (in this

[1] Jn. 15,4.

case the blow on our face) and our reaction to it. This is the moment which gives us the opportunity to reap the fruit of the two previous stages of the exercise in which our mind has been informed by, and our heart has tasted of, Omnipotence. In this third stage, by learning to *do* something by the Omnipotence of I AM, we actually grow in spiritual stature.[1] This moment really determines whether we, and to the extent that we are part of it the whole corporeal realm, remain in the natural state or undergo some measure of transformation into the supra-natural state. And since the Spirit is universal, this transformation is not confined to the corporeal realm merely as represented by our own selves, but has its effects upon corporeal creation throughout all space and time.[2]

The moment we feel the furious impulse to retaliate to the blow on our face, if possible even before, we must try to recall the watchword as vividly as possible. "I AM . . . the Almighty". The more painful the blow, the more violent our reaction is likely to be, and the harder it will be to recall the watchword vividly enough to evoke the whole Saying with the Divine Feeling enshrined in it. The more painful the blow, the more tempted we shall be to use our will to suppress our counterblow on ethical grounds. Let us once more remember that if we use our will like this, we misuse it for spiritual purposes and waste the exercise by acting on the moral and not the spiritual plane. By thus acting without I AM, we *do* nothing in the full sense, achieve nothing, because our violence and its parent root the fallen self remain essentially unimpaired, and therefore ready to erupt on future occasions. We not only fail to grow spiritually ourselves, but fail to do anything creative for our opponent. He remains hostile. At this critical point, when tempted to retaliate, or even to suppress the temptation to retaliate, it can be very helpful to recall another Saying: "Not by might, nor by power, but by MY Spirit".[3]

Let it be stressed for the last time that we use our will *creatively* only in keeping our attention fixed upon the watchword, so as to lead to our surrender to the Saying to do its work in us. Only so do we allow the Spirit of Him Who utters it to work creatively in us. If

[1] Phil. 4,13; Eph. 4,13 & 15.
[2] Rom. 8,22.
[3] Zech. 4,6.

our impulse is violent enough, we may have to repeat the watchword as fast as possible, almost in a whisper. Even if this does not immediately evoke the whole Saying, it will prevent the impulse from working itself out in the counterblow. If we then persevere, we are sooner or later bound to get the watchword in clear and vivid focus, from where it is comparatively easy to begin mentally repeating the whole Saying.

As this is the last exercise to be described in detail, and will therefore have to serve as a rough guide for the design of others, we had better consider how its intensity can be increased as the capacity to surrender to Sayings grows. There are obviously direct links between the stimuli we meet, the force of the fallen self's reaction, and our strength of will to focus attention on the watchword and Saying. As that strength develops, it is necessary to imagine increasingly powerful stimuli and correspondingly forceful reactions by our fallen self. Without this, the exercises sooner or later cease to be of much use in stimulating our spiritual growth. In the case we are describing, for instance, we may imagine ourselves provoked with increasing severity, the blow on the face injuring the eye, accompanied with an insulting expletive. And so on. At every step we imagine the reaction which our self-knowledge leads us to expect from our fallen self. The next chapter will suggest how exercises may be devised by imagining different situations with a view to attacking other points of our fallen self.

It is of course necessary to avoid flights of fancy in imagining unrealistically powerful stimuli or forceful reactions, which would merely distract us from our training. We should soberly and realistically increase our imagined difficulties as the growing strength of our will permits us to surrender to the Sayings. So we genuinely train ourselves to meet the temptations of real life, whose overcoming is the very growing point of our spiritual stature. It cannot be overstressed that we cannot grow spiritually without trial, as though in a void. Every time we overcome a trial or temptation by the Spirit of a Saying and therefore of I AM, the natural force of the reaction which fails to discharge itself is transmuted into spiritual Power. The classic instance is the triple temptation which Jesus overcame in the wilderness. According to S. Matthew, the devil on being rejected left Jesus for the time being and was replaced by ministering angels.[1] In other words, the force of the natural reaction, on being overcome, was transmuted into spiritual Power.

This transmutation progresses most rapidly, of course, when actual trials or temptations are spiritually overcome. But the imagined overcoming of imagined trials, if practised properly, clearly also has some transmuting effect, although it is of course slower. In fact, since actual trials are insuperable without spiritual training, the main difference between the real and the imagined ones is in the rate of spiritual growth they afford.

As our preparation for the last Silence has been interrupted by suggestions for devising further exercises, we had better recapitulate the crucial point of the present one, where we are strongly tempted to react naturally to the blow on the face. We therefore return to our study and face our enemy. He makes his demand. We reject it. He loses his temper, swings back his arm and hits us hard and painfully in the face. We feel the furious impulse of our fallen self surging up in us to hit him back harder. We feel the civilised impulse to inhibit the natural one, but reject it. We imagine the anger rising to the degree at which it is about matched by the strength of our will to recall the watchword. "I AM . . . the Almighty". We go on mentally repeating it until it holds our attention. We make the further effort of will necessary to recall the whole Saying and try to taste the Divine Feeling with which it is charged. "I AM . . . the Beginning and the Ending . . . the Almighty".

In order to taste the Feeling as richly as possible, and avoid confusing force with Power, we draw on every aid. We recall that Power derives from Wisdom which derives from Love. If necessary, we recall our experience in the course of administering the Sacraments of the Holy Eucharist, Penance and Baptism. It may pass through our mind that if a baby had hit us in the face in the course of being baptised, we would have felt no urge to retaliate. Let us suppose that these aids, recalled in a flash, enable us to taste something of the Omnipotence of I AM. It is borne in on us that if His Loving, Understanding Knowledge of the scowling face before us were to falter even for a moment, that face and the self it masks would vanish instantly as though it had never been. It cannot falter even for a moment. For His Love, Wisdom and Power are the primal

[1] Mat. 4,11.

qualities of His Will, Heart and Mind. If He faltered in His Love, Wisdom and Power, therefore, He would deny Himself.[1] Moreover, since the scowling face before us no more than fleetingly masks a differentiated aspect of His SELF, He would diminish His all-inclusive wholeness by thus faltering. Which is inconceivable because He includes all that is or can be knowable. So in surrendering to the Saying, we awaken to the indwelling presence of I AM as the Source, Ground and Goal of *all* things, including ourselves and our enemy.

With our will now attuned to express the Saying, we are ready for the Silence. Fixing our eyes on our enemy's eyes, we begin mentally repeating the Saying, until we are aware only of I AM Whose eternal Utterance it is. Abiding in Him, and He in us, it is out of our hands to choose how to act, or speak, or even look at the man. He ceases to be our enemy. For in that moment, in some degree, "we are dead, and our life is hid with Christ in God".[2] In that degree I AM "dwells and walks in us".[3] The self of our late enemy is one with our self and all things in The SELF. "There is none else".[4] We, who are heirs of God, have for that moment in some degree entered into our Supreme Inheritance.[5]

"I AM . . . the Beginning and the Ending . . . the Almighty".

Ten to fifteen minutes' silence.

The last Silence ends, as always, with the simple thanksgiving and self-oblation described in the previous exercises.

---

[1] 2 Tim. 2,13.
[2] Col. 3,3.
[3] 2 Cor. 6,16.
[4] Isa. 45,14.
[5] Rom. 8,17; Num. 18,20.

Chapter 10

The Use of Divine Power

[1]

We have exercised ourselves in using the Power of I AM to overcome one particular difficulty, and thus to *do* one particular thing through Him. Let us suppose that the warden has not remained unaffected by his last encounter with us, and has now offered us his willing co-operation. The thing we have in some degree managed to *get done* therefore is, by ourselves being purged of a weakness which has brought down upon us a man's bitter hostility, to create a friend out of an enemy. This is a tiny instance of corporeal men's creative work of transforming the jungle of the natural world into the City and ultimately the Temple of God. And, as we have seen, he can do it only by his weakness being made perfect by the Power of I AM.

Once we have learned to use this Power to *do* one thing, we can and should plan further exercises in *doing* other things by the same means. It is unnecessary to set these out in detail if the pattern of the previous exercises is followed. On the contrary, nothing impresses the principles underlying the incarnation of I AM in ourselves more clearly than to plan and carry out our own exercises. If necessary, the help of someone more experienced may be sought, but the sooner this is dispensed with the better. For ultimately our salvation, which lies in the fulfilment of our destiny through union with I AM, can only be worked out by ourselves.[1] It may therefore be of help if we summarise the main points to be borne in mind in devising our own exercises.

The most important point is that the Power of I AM is but the creative aspect of His SELF and is inseparable from the other facets, attributes and values of His Personality. Having split this up, as it were, for purposes of study and training, we are always liable to

---

[1] Ps. 35,3; Phil. 2,12.

the danger of forgetting that I AM is indivisible as the supreme Triunity. His Power lies in the True Knowing of His Mind, His All-consciousness, which derives from the Mysterious Wisdom of His Heart, which in turn derives from the Loving Goodness of His Will. In other words, these three facets of His Personality are His SELF in course of willing, feeling and knowing all things, whereby He *is* the knowable Reality in its subjective and objective aspects.

This leads us to the next point to be borne in mind. We have seen that His Power lies in His Knowledge of all things, whereby they are created, upheld and fulfilled. We may therefore say that He *uses* His Power by means of His Thoughts, as signified by His Sayings. "As I have thought, so shall it come to pass", He therefore declares; "as I have spoken now, so shall it come to pass".[1] It follows that whoever aspires to use the Power of I AM as He uses it can only do so in so far as he possesses, *has,* embodies His Sayings. For only so can he embody the Mind of I AM by the Power of which He creates, upholds and fulfils all things. The aspirant must therefore acquire the fullest possible vocabulary of the Sayings signifying the Omnipotent Thoughts by which I AM does all things.

This means first that the aspirant must know the Bible well enough to pick out these Sayings in their significance as he needs them to use Divine Power. But he will not acquire his "Divine Vocabulary" by merely running through the Bible in order to compile a list of Sayings, for these will then have little significance for him, like foreign phrases without a translation. He will have to study the Bible devotionally, and "wait upon" I AM to reveal His Sayings to him one by one as he becomes spiritually fit to grasp their significance. These revelations are unmistakable. The Saying leaps out from the page like a secret cypher suddenly made plain. He will therefore build up his "Divine Vocabulary" as a child learns to speak. Spiritually he is a child growing up "unto the measure of the stature of the fulness of Christ".[2]

Having been given the Sayings as he becomes *fit* to receive them, the aspirant must then go on to receive them so as to possess, *have,* embody them. The next point to be borne in mind is the sequence and method by which their embodiment takes place most directly.

---

[1] Isa. 14,24; 2 Esdras 8,40.
[2] Eph. 4,13.

They become embodied so that they themselves *work* in the aspirant only in so far as he first receives them in his mind, then assimilates them with his heart, and finally expresses them by the proper use of his will. And the method by which he achieves this is to let them dwell in him as richly as possible. Having done his best to attune his mind, heart and will as described in the previous chapters, he must resolutely put away his own resources as useless irrelevancies, and let nothing but the "spiritual milk" of the Sayings feed him.[1]

The last point to be borne in mind concerns the selection of the Sayings from the "Divine Vocabulary" we are building up. This was a relatively simple matter in the case of the four exercises already described. Starting from scratch, we offered ourselves like a photographic film for the Will, Heart and Mind of I AM to be imprinted upon us.[2] We had therefore only to select four Sayings which seemed best to signify the Unity and the three facets of the Triunity of I AM. But now that we have in some degree, however small, embodied these three facets of His SELF and aspire to *do* things through His Love, Wisdom and Power, the selection of the Sayings requires more consideration.

Our need for Power comes home to us most vividly through our difficulties. It should be plain to us by now that these do not come upon us by chance, but exactly correspond with the stage we have reached in our spiritual growth. We draw them upon us by the strong points of our fallen self, so that the resulting suffering may stimulate us to cut off the offending excrescences.[3] Or conversely, we draw them upon us by the weak points of our awakening True Self, so that we may be driven to seek Power to strengthen them. So the Power of I AM is made perfect in weakness, as He Himself declares to S. Paul.[4] Our difficulties and sufferings are thus the purifying discipline we precisely need to perfect our expression of the Glory of God in corporeal terms.[5] Ultimately they are God-sent, as I AM on many occasions declares. "This thing is of ME . . . I have done these things unto thee . . . It is a terrible thing that I

---

[1] Phil. 3,8 RV; 1 Pet. 2,3 RV.
[2] 2 Cor. 3,18 RV.
[3] Mat. 18,8.
[4] 2 Cor. 12,9 RV.
[5] Heb. 2,10.

do with thee".[1]   Nor does He leave His purpose in doing so in any doubt.   His Love moves Him to discipline man, He declares, so that man might partake of His Holiness.[2]   And without that man cannot attain the supreme satisfaction of fulfilling his destiny by expressing the Glory of God in corporeal terms.

It follows from this that the Sayings we must first select for our further exercises are those which enable us to overcome difficulties attracted to us by our crudest weaknesses.   This demands as objective an assessment of our spiritual condition as we can make.   So we become able to take part with increasing intelligence in the self-expressive work of I AM in and through us.   It is as though the clay in the sculptor's hands, which begins by being intractable and indeed recalcitrant material, learns first not to hinder his movements and then to cooperate.   Ultimately the image comes to life, and in union with its creator carries out his purpose itself.[3]

If man must fall from his pristine innocence in order to recover and possess it as his holiness, as we have already seen, sin and suffering clearly play an indispensable part in his journey towards the fulfilment of his destiny.   In the abstract, our mind may not find it hard to grasp the nature and purpose of error, ugliness and evil, the three main aspects of sin, in the course of this journey.   It is only as our heart follows the mind, and we come to assess our spiritual condition with passionless objectivity, that we become able to understand the purpose of our own particular sins and sufferings.   This is perhaps the point, to return to our illustration of the image of clay, at which it comes to life and begins actively to cooperate with its maker.   At this point we are sufficiently attuned to the standpoint of I AM to lose all doubt that He forgives our sins, takes the ultimate responsibility for them upon His SELF, and atones for them by suffering all the suffering they cause.[4]   For since we are differentiated aspects of His SELF, He ultimately does so for His Own sake.   If He did not, His self-unfoldment through Corporeal Man would be frustrated, and the Glory of God would not be expressed.   "I, even I, AM He that blotteth out thy transgressions for MINE Own sake", He declares.   "For MY Name's sake . . . I cut thee not off . . . for

---

[1] 1 Kgs. 12,24; Jer. 30,15 RV; Ex. 34,10 RV.
[2] Heb. 12,10.
[3] Collect for Lent I; Isa. 45,9; Isa. 64,8.
[4] Isa. 63,9.

MINE Own sake, will I do it; for how should MY Name be polluted?"[1] Perhaps it is only then that we really accept our suffering as the pain which is inseparable from all creation, and without which its joy is impossible.[2] For we now *take part* in the creative work on the raw material, the clay, represented by our fallen selves. As we come to recognise the transformation of the jungle of the natural world, which includes the fallen self, into the City and Temple of God as the greatest creative work that is conceivable, so we no longer merely endure but meet its pain for the sake of the joy it brings.[3]

It remains for us to give the simplest possible example of assessing our spiritual condition, selecting the Saying which corrects the weakness we regard as most prominent at the time, and devising an exercise to suit the case. Let us suppose that we recognise the weakness most urgently needing correction in us as a rather subtle anxiety. It concerns not ourselves but our ministry, and springs from our failure to draw people in trouble to ourselves for help. The more troubled we are thereby, of course, the less likely people in trouble are to come to us, if only because we lack the serenity which they themselves lack. Our immediate need is to receive some Saying from our "Divine Vocabulary" which will give us the Spirit of Divine Serenity. The Power of I AM having been made perfect in this particular weakness of ours, we shall then be able to pass on the gift to others.

There are many Sayings through which we could receive the Spirit of Divine Serenity. The more accurately we diagnose our anxiety, the more able we are to select the Saying which exactly fits our need. If, for instance, our anxiety springs from insecurity, from an inadequate certainty of being upheld by I AM, we need a Saying assuring us of His unswerving faithfulness. "I will not fail thee, nor forsake thee", is one of many to the same effect.[4] But let us suppose that our anxiety is less rational and more deep-seated, being a lack of inner peace having no objective cause. The Saying which best

---

[1] Isa. 43,25; Isa. 48,9 & 11 AV & RV combined.
[2] Heb. 2,12.
[3] Heb. 12,2.
[4] Josh. 1,5.

supplies our lack may then be one in which I AM plainly signifies the gift of His own Peace to us. "My Peace I give unto you".[1]

Having selected the Saying most suited to our need, we go on to design an exercise in three stages to enable us to receive the Spirit of the Saying in our mind, assimilate it with our heart, and express it by our will. Each stage consists first of a brief meditation designed to attune mind, heart and will in turn to the Saying, and then of a Silence of ten or more minutes. The Silence is of course the most vital part of each stage in which the effort to receive, assimilate and express the Saying actually takes place, and in which its Spirit becomes embodied accordingly. Since the exercise is based on what we regard as the way in which The SELF most directly becomes incarnate in our selves, its three stages should be set out in a little more detail, however familiar these may be from the preceding chapters.

We begin the first stage with a meditation on the Saying with a view to attuning our mind to it. We marshal our theological knowledge of Divine Peace and of the manner in which I AM gives it to us. The mind thus attuned, we adopt the proper posture for the Silence and devote two minutes to answering His call to come to Him with all our burdens, especially any due to our lack of Peace. Then we turn from our fallen self and all its thoughts, and concentrate our whole attention on the Saying. "MY Peace I give unto you". We continue mentally repeating this for ten or more minutes, seeking to know Him within us as He gives His Peace to us.

The second stage begins with a meditation on the feeling content of the Saying so as to attune our heart to the Divine Feeling with which it is charged. That Feeling being ineffable, our meditation can only point us towards it. Some priestly experience in the course of performing an office may do this best, as described in the foregoing chapters. Then follows the second Silence of ten or more minutes during which the Saying is mentally repeated as before, but with attention focussed upon the Feeling enshrined in it. So the Feeling gently distils into the sum total of our experience.

The last stage consists in exercising our will to express the Saying in action, by using our imagination. We begin by reviewing some actual situation in which we shall be called upon to help someone

---

[1] Jn. 14,27.

168

in trouble to find peace. The greatest peace, indeed the only true peace they can find is the Peace of I AM. If we surrender to the Saying in which He gives us His Peace, and let it work in us, we can become a channel of His Peace to the person in trouble. Before we can do this with real effect in the actual situation, we need practice in the coming Silence. We therefore imagine the sufferer as clearly as possible, and then concentrate our whole attention on the Saying. Mentally repeating it, we seek to be one with I AM Who utters it, yet without losing contact with the sufferer. In the degree that we succeed, the Peace of I AM goes out to him through us. In making ourselves a channel of Divine Peace, we give him that Peace in the Name of I AM.

We end the last Silence with some words of thanksgiving and self-oblation. This should include the determination to practise the exercise every day for a month, or whatever period our self-knowledge tells us is necessary if we are to embody some appreciable degree of Divine Peace. As mentioned before, in the daily practice of the exercise its successive stages should be combined as quickly as possible so that the last sums them all up. We need not of course have the same sufferer in mind each day, or indeed anyone but ourselves. For before we can be a channel of Peace to others, we must first have it ourselves. In practice, therefore, the daily exercise should usually consist of two or more Silences in which we recall our difficulties and then try to receive Peace in mind, heart and will simultaneously. No less important is the constant use of a watchword, especially as we fall asleep and wake up.

[2]

The exercises set out in this book are of value in their own right as means of spiritual growth. But their main value obviously consists in fitting us to use the Power of I AM — by giving Peace in His Name to others for instance — in every day life in which difficulties are actual and not imaginary. We must therefore end this chapter, which is concerned with the use of Divine Power in general, by touching on two chief modes in which we may *do* things through I AM, or in His Name. These two modes are due to our humanity being both spiritual and corporeal. The two modes are thus interrelated and difficult to label accurately, but we might call them visible and invisible according to the factor which is most in evidence. In these exercises we are primarily concerned with the use of spiritual power by priests, but its use by others cannot differ in principle.

We begin with the visible mode. The parish priest is responsible for the spiritual welfare of the people within his parish boundaries, or other spheres in this world, and in that sense has charge of them. Now these human beings are essentially differentiated aspects of The SELF, as their priest is. This charge must therefore be laid on him because he should be, at least potentially, more aware of The SELF as his True Self than on the whole they are. The very reason for which he is given charge of other selves determines the manner in which alone he can truly discharge his responsibility. He can only do so by using the Power of I AM which derives from His Wisdom which derives from His Love. In other words, his power or authority rests essentially on his ability to understand his people, and this in turn rests on his will to spend himself for their welfare.

His sphere of responsibility may therefore be seen as a tiny fief which I AM has called him to rule in His Name, in other words, to rule as He Himself rules the spiritual realm and (through mankind) the corporeal realm. Since terrestrial mankind in this age is still very much learning the art of exercising supreme sovereignty, and is still very far from "reigning with Christ for ever", the priest's sphere of responsibility may also be seen as a training ground.[1] It is probably very much harder for any secular ruler in this age to regard his sphere of responsibility in this light. This draws attention again to the extraordinary privilege conferred by priesthood. Also to the penalties which must inevitably follow on failure to fulfil the corresponding responsibilities in the Name of I AM. Any parish priest who tries to rule in his own name pays for his failure as no secular ruler does.[2]

In previous chapters we saw certain priestly acts as an earthly counterpart of that which I AM eternally does spiritually. The whole priestly life is ideally such a counterpart, and so foreshadows the life of all mankind called to "the priesthood of all believers".

Since the parish priest can fulfil his many-sided charge solely by

[1] 2 Tim. 2,12; Rev. 5,10; Rev. 22,5.
[2] Lk. 12,48.

the Power of I AM, it follows that he must seek it not only in the general sense of empowering him to *do* anything whatever, but in its particular form demanded by different occasions. Obviously the first essential is to start the day by seeking the ability to *do* anything whatever in the Name of I AM. The next is to seek His Power in the form needed to *do* some particular thing, such as to give Peace in His Name. The proper time to start seeking Power in the general sense is at the moment of awaking. In the exercises set out here, we do this by recalling the watchword and Saying we have chosen to signify I AM as the Almighty. "I AM . . . the Beginning and the Ending . . . the Almighty". The early Silence of the day should follow as soon as possible after awaking, and certainly before becoming involved in the affairs of the day. The importance of attuning mind, heart and will to the Sayings has repeatedly been mentioned. Also that the three stages of receiving the Sayings should be combined as soon as possible. As it is particularly important to ensure a sound preparation for the first Silence of the day in which Power in its general sense is sought, an example of such a combination may be helpful.

The best way of ensuring that the essential ground is covered is to recall what has been called the "formula", which should possess much more significance now than when first set out in chapter 5, owing to the experience gained in the exercises set out in the subsequent chapters. For this formula seeks to represent the Loving Will, the Wise Heart and the Intellectual Power in which I AM does all things whatsoever, as their Source, Ground and Goal. If we can recall the formula every morning, we begin to build into our thinking, feeling and activity the whole pattern of the creative self-unfoldment of I AM, as He fills Heaven and Earth, and thereby attune our mind, heart and will in combination to the Saying with increasing speed and sureness. When the formula has been built into us and we know it as well as our own name, so that we can for instance recall it when woken at night, we can reduce it to its barest essentials as represented by the few Sayings upon which it is based. For we shall understand these Sayings well enough to begin drawing out their all-inclusive significance without the aid of the rest of the formula. These three essential Sayings are as follows.

"I AM God . . . the Holy One in the midst of thee. I fill Heaven and Earth. I AM . . . the Beginning and the Ending . . . the Almighty".

So with increasing brevity, speed and sureness we learn to attune our mind, heart and will to the last of these three Sayings, which signifies the Power of I AM by which He does all things. We also learn to look for that Power as coming forth from the "midst of us", that is from the hidden depth beyond the summit of our self in its most aware state. Then we enter the Silence in which we receive that Power, and therefore the ability to *do* anything whatever during the coming day. We begin the Silence as always by allowing two minutes in which to respond to the call to come to I AM with all our burdens. Then we still our fallen self, turn from it, renounce it, and concentrate on the mental repetition of the Saying. "I AM . . . the Beginning and the Ending . . . the Almighty". At the end of the Silence we give thanks for the Power we have received, offer our emptied self to be filled by His SELF, and resolve to remain in that state by recalling the watchword and Saying as often as possible throughout the coming day. "I AM . . . the Almighty".

We turn next to the second essential, the actual *use* of Divine Power for any particular purpose during the day, such as to give Peace in His Name to someone in trouble. We can do this, of course, only in so far as we possess His Peace ourselves. If our self-assessment reveals our lack of it, we must take time for a Silence in order to receive it before our interview with the sufferer. We may use the Saying already mentioned: "MY Peace I give unto you". Or the sufferer's particular needs may lead us to select another from the "Divine Vocabulary" we are building up.

At this point someone new to the method of spiritual training we are outlining may perhaps begin to lose patience. How is he, if a busy parish priest, to find time and energy to prepare himself to act in the Name of I AM in so many different particular ways? If this is the case, it should be remembered that Divine Power, which is universal, can be used to the best effect in the corporeal realm only in particular ways. Without this particularisation, Divine Power is akin to undirected energy. Therefore, if he is not prepared to train himself by some method to use Divine Power to the best effect, he must resign himself to acting in the Name of I AM only in a very general sense.

Whoever hopes to be a true minister, vassal, disciple of I AM in fact as well as in name really has no alternative but somehow to train himself to use the Power of I AM, and therefore truly act in His Name, in increasingly various particular ways. Only thereby does he really advance towards the point of doing *all* particular things through I AM.[1] A heavily engaged priest probably finds it possible to train himself to act in the Name of I AM only on the most critical occasions in his ministry, say, when the gift of Divine Peace is desperately needed. He soon knows, not only in theory but by experience, the abysmal distinction between work done in his own name and in the Name of I AM. With practice a few seconds' Silence, the mere recollection of the Saying, of the watchword alone as he welcomes the sufferer in need of Peace, will enable him to draw on its Divine Source and give it away in the boundless Love, Wisdom and Power of I AM.

In the light of one such experience, he will soon begin to widen the area in which he really *does* things and not merely churns water. As the Power of I AM is thus made perfect in his various weaknesses and he learns to do more things in His Name, he will require less preparation for each occasion. For in building up his "Divine Vocabulary" of Sayings and working to embody their Spirit, he will increasingly "put on" The SELF Who does all things whatsoever both universally and particularly. The use of Divine Power in particular ways is essentially the application of the universal to particular ends, which is the purpose for which Corporeal Man is created, and without which he cannot manifest the Glory of the Holy One in corporeal terms.

[3]

Having touched on what we have called the visible mode of using Divine Power, we end the chapter by touching on the invisible mode. This is the mode in which I AM directly rules the spiritual realm and indirectly, through corporeal mankind, the corporeal realm. We have called this mode invisible because it does not depend upon immediate personal contact between individuals, and it may be said to begin with what is usually called one person's intercession for another,

[1] Phil. 4,13.

though we shall not use the term at first in order to avoid confusion with its conventional connotation.

However large any person's sphere of responsibility may be on this earth, it cannot include more than a small part of terrestrial society, which is itself a microscopic part of that which spreads over the whole corporeal realm. Whoever aspires to progress towards the fulfilment of the ultimate purpose of his existence, which is to serve and thus rule both the spiritual and corporeal realms through the Power of I AM, to "reign with Him for ever", must therefore fit himself for translation to a wider sphere than he is at any time responsible for. I AM incarnate makes it clear in a parable that this will not come about until the aspirant has learned to rule in His Name in a smaller sphere.[1] The reason for this is plain when we recall what translation essentially involves.

When we consider a man's ability to use the Power of I AM in order to *do* an increasing number of things through Him, or in His Name, we find that this is merely another way of describing his awakening to The SELF as his True Self. As he thus grows spiritually, he cannot help becoming aware of greater spheres of responsibility open to him. (The whole knowable Reality is The SELF's sphere of responsibility). As a man learns to give himself for these spheres as they open out to him, and to understand them, he receives the power to rule over them. So they become his, bought by his self-sacrifice, a series of increasingly great fiefs to be ruled in the Name of I AM. His spiritual awakening may be seen as the subjective aspect of his translation to greater spheres of spiritual responsibility. He may thus be said, in that sense, to translate himself as his self grows towards the stature of The SELF and he becomes spiritually fit to rule greater spheres. For as he awakens to The SELF as his True Self, and thereby moves towards the all-consciousness of Him Who is the whole knowable Reality, he sees these spheres awaiting his ministry. As he progressively inherits I AM, he comes to see Divine Sovereignty as his in I AM. So he advances towards the fulfilment of his destiny, which is the Sovereignty or Kingdom of Heaven and Earth.

The more clearly a man sees the ultimate purpose of his existence, the more directly he is bound to pursue it. All other pursuits drop

[1] Lk. 19,17.

away from him because they cease for him to be reasonable, interesting and satisfying. To be exact, the more time and energy he cannot help devoting to the invisible use of Divine Power in the increasingly great spheres of responsibility opening out before him. As a void to be filled, they call to him to give himself for their sake, to understand them and thus to rule them. The obvious beginning in this invisible use of Divine Power is in satisfying the needs of people personally known to him. Let us illustrate this by continuing our previous example of a person who asks for help to receive Divine Peace, but without a personal interview. In conventional language, he asks for prayer to be made on his behalf for Peace.

Since we can do nothing without I AM, we must obviously begin by receiving His Peace ourselves before trying to give it to the sufferer in His Name. (Hence all conventional intercession is made through, or in the Name of God, i.e. Christ). As in our previous illustration, we choose the Saying that best suits the need, and try to receive its Spirit of Peace as deeply as possible. Then we clearly visualise the sufferer and his need for Peace. We thereby become a channel between him and I AM in us, as though taking him with us into the indwelling presence of The SELF. We can obviously take him no further into I AM, as it were, than we ourselves have been able to ascend. Nor can we give him more Peace than we ourselves have received.[1] Having thus become a channel between him and the only Source of true Peace, we devote the remaining time we have set aside for this intercession to the mental repetition of the Saying, seeking to transmit the gift of Peace to the sufferer as we receive it. It is as though we made ourselves into a hand-mirror to transmit sunlight upon some dark spot.

I AM declares that when He is in the world, He is the Light of the world.[2] He informs human society in the corporeal realm only in so far as He is embodied in men. We may infer from this that there is Light in the world, that is to say All-consciousness, only in so far as His Will, Heart and Mind as expressed by His Sayings enlightens human thinking, feeling and activity. This reminds us again of the crucial importance of our spiritual growth, not only for

---

[1] Jas. 5,16.
[2] Jn. 9,5 RV.

175

our own sake, but for the sake of the world. Hence Jesus declared that He sanctified Himself for the sake of His disciples, and prayed that they in turn might be sanctified through the Word of God.[1]

If this transmitting of Light is to grow in effectiveness, it is obviously no easy art to acquire, and a little more practical detail on the subject may be of use. As we mentally repeat the Saying which *is* the Spirit of Peace, our attention must be primarily fixed upon I AM within us as He gives us His Peace, and only secondarily upon the sufferer to whom Peace goes forth through us. We must not become entangled in the sufferer's problems in any detail. I AM alone knows them perfectly, as well as their solution. They are indeed no problems to Him, as there is no darkness in light.[2] We must be aware of the sufferer only as in need of Divine Peace. As we continue mentally repeating the Saying, in the degree that we cease to be aware of ourselves and become one with I AM, we know only His Peace as He gives it to the sufferer. This is the most fruitful stage of the intercession, in which we most truly act in the Name of I AM, and through Him bring forth the fruit of His Peace in the sufferer.[3] Hence this stage should occupy the greatest part of the intercession. It should always end with a short act of thanksgiving that the gift of Peace has indeed gone forth to the sufferer.[4]

This very simple instance of the invisible use of Divine Power for the welfare of another, whereby he is to that extent "ruled" in the Name of I AM, has been described in some detail in order to bring out its essentials. If these are borne in mind, we can consider a more elaborate instance without overstepping our available space. The subject is literally endless, since it includes all conceivable human needs as well as the unsearchable riches of I AM which are superabundantly able to satisfy them. The following instance concerns the invisible use of Divine Power in a sphere which consists of selves who are not known to us personally and whose needs are more complex than one for Divine Peace.

Let us suppose that some branch of the "Church militant here in earth" is undergoing sufficient persecution to ask especially for intercession, as has often happened in the present age. If we are to

[1] Jn. 17,17 & 19.
[2] 1 Jn. 1,5.
[3] Jn. 15,5.
[4] Jn. 11,41

make the most intelligent use of Divine Power in order to give this help, we must ascertain two essential facts. One is the most pressing need of the persecuted Church; the particular weakness it is aware of in its trial. The other is the particular aspect of the unsearchable riches of I AM which will best satisfy this need; the particular form of His Power which will be made perfect in that weakness.

Let us suppose that the Church is bewildered by its difficulties, fails to appreciate fully their ultimate reason, and that the faith of many of its members is shaken. We turn to I AM within for guidance, and are led to the conclusion that the most fruitful way of satisfying this need is to transmit to the persecuted Church His assurance of Faithfulness and Protection, under all conceivable conditions and circumstances. Still led by I AM, we search the Bible, or more easily our "Divine Vocabulary" *if it is large enough,* for the Saying which will best signify His assurance to the persecuted Church in its specific difficulties. No single Saying, it may be, reveals itself as quite fitting the rather complex need. Let us suppose that we are led to the following series of Sayings, arranged in the order which fits the need best.

"MY People . . . which I formed for MYSELF, that they might set forth MY Praise. MY chosen . . . shall be tried as the gold in the fire . . . refined . . . in the furnace of affliction. Fear thou not; for I AM with thee: be not dismayed. Abide in ME, and I in you. Ye shall be Holy; for I AM Holy".[1]

At first sight the use of such a series of Sayings seems formidable. Their selection alone might be thought to take a long time. But whoever knows the Bible thoroughly, has built up an adequate "Divine Vocabulary", and above all constantly recollects the indwelling presence of I AM, will find the Sayings required to satisfy the need put into his mind almost as he sets out to seek them. For the same reason the preparation of the mind, heart and will to receive the Spirit of a series of Sayings will take him very little longer than in the case of a single one. As always, there can be no substitute for the constant and devoted practice by which alone he gradually comes to *have* the Mind of Christ, in S. Paul's language.

Let us suppose that, with mind, heart and will attuned to this

[1] Isa. 43,20 & 21 RV; 2 Esdras 16,73; Isa. 48,10; Isa. 41,10; Jn. 15,4; Lev. 11,44.

series of Sayings, we are now ready for the Silence in which our intercession for the persecuted Church is to be made. Since we can pass on nothing we have not received, we must first do our best to receive the Spirit of Faithfulness and Protection enshrined in these Sayings. We begin mentally repeating them, letting them dwell in us as richly as possible in order to embody their Spirit, precisely as we would a single Saying. Very soon the series will come to be represented by one of its component Sayings, or perhaps by a part of that one. We make no choice in this. It is given to us which to choose, in the degree that we become one with I AM Who utters them. What actually happens is that the Words we need remain in our mind, and the rest drop away. The Words thus given to us may be: "Abide in ME, and I in you". Or they may be: "Ye shall be Holy; for I AM Holy". As we come to abide in I AM, we remember the leaders and members of the persecuted Church. Having established this link between them and I AM in us, we fix our whole attention on I AM within us as His assurance of Faithfulness and Protection pours forth to the sufferers.

Space does not allow us to give further instances of the invisible use of Divine Power. The endless possibilities of this use can only be dealt with by discussion with one more experienced. The scope of these possibilities may be seen when we consider the use of Divine Power to serve human needs, not only in this world and this age, but in all worlds, in all ages, in all conditions.

Whoever aspires to serve, thereby rule, and thus make his own the whole corporeal realm will have to learn as a first step to intercede for it in Spirit and in Truth on this universal scale. For, as we have seen, it is his growing concern for its welfare that marks his spiritual growth, his awakening to The SELF as his True Self. So he moves towards the ultimate purpose of his existence, the sovereignty in The SELF of the whole spiritual as well as corporeal realms. Eternally living and reigning in Him and with Him, he then *constitutes* both these aspects of the knowable Reality. One with I AM, he *is* all that ever has been, is, or will be knowable.[1] It is towards this consummation that all corporeal mankind is moving and, from the all-comprehending standpoint of I AM, has already attained. Heaven and Earth *are* full of His Glory.

[1] Jn. 17,24; 1 Cor. 13,12; 1 Jn. 3,2; Rev. 22,4.

Index of Biblical References